lighthouses

lighthouses

JACKUM BROWN

CASSELL ILLUSTRATED

First published in Great Britain in 2005 by Cassell
Illustrated, a division of Octopus Publishing Group
Limited, 2—4 Heron Quays, London E14 4JP.

Design and layout copyright © 2005 Octopus
Publishing Group Limited.

Text copyright © 2005 Jackum Brown.

A CIP catalogue record for this book is available
from the British Library.

ISBN 1-84403-341-4
EAN 9781844033416

Editor: Joanne Wilson
Design: Design 23

Printed at Toppan, China

Previous page: **Nantucket Island, Massachussets.**

Left: **St Ives, Cornwall.**

contents

Lighthouses are extraordinary structures.

They hold a place in the human heart that no other type of building can match. Perched on headlands or on rocky outcrops at sea, pounded by waves and battered by winds, their lights shine out, pointing towards the heavens, offering the gifts of safety, security, hope, hearth and home to those courageous people who leave the land in search of food, knowledge and new discoveries.

There is something deeply romantic about lighthouses, and the people who have lived and worked in them have been the subjects of local legends and countless mariners songs and sea shanties. It must be an extremely lonely life to be a lighthouse keeper, as well as a very tough existence, and yet people all over the world have dedicated themselves to keeping the lights lit, in order to help preserve the lives of strangers.

We admire and respect those who have worked and still work in lighthouses. We salute their sense of duty and purpose, and not least their ability to live their lives in an often hostile environment, with little human contact. Part of us envies these men and women for their inner strength and their capacity to live and thrive in such circumstances, while at the same time we recognize that most of us could not possibly do it ourselves.

Lighthouses seem to have a unique quality that makes us both love and revere them. Of course, we love our own homes, admire our national monuments and gaze in awe at astonishing feats of engineering, both ancient and modern – Egyptian and Mayan

INTRODUCTION

pyramids, Greek temples, Roman ruins, bridges, cathedrals, castles and skyscrapers can all grab our attention. However, those who live near lighthouses usually feel proud – even quite possessive – of them, and often come together to put up a fight if those in authority wish to dispose of them.

Each lighthouse is special, a labour of love, whether built hundreds of years ago or more recently. Lighthouses are designed and decorated differently all over the world. To the casual observer, these decorations seem like eccentricities. Why should some lighthouses be painted with a black and white diamond pattern as opposed to a red and white candy stripe? Why did snowy Canada decide on the 'pepperpot' design, and so often paint its lighthouses white with red lanterns or white with red doors, when the equally snowy Iceland painted many of its lighthouses orange? There seems to be neither rhyme nor reason to their appearance, and yet their own intrinsic individuality – as well as the individuality of their designers and builders – seems to be just another thing for which to love them.

Hundreds of years ago, people were prepared to risk their lives and their health, over several years at a time, to build the great rock lighthouses in the sea. Many of these lighthouses still stand today, albeit using modern technology such as electronic systems and solar power (Trinity House, the organization that looks after lighthouses in Britain, is the greatest user of solar power in the country). It is hard to imagine that there was a time when candles and, before them, open fires, produced the light that saved people's lives.

East Quoddy lighthouse,
New Brunswick,
Canada.

The invention of the global positioning system (GPS) seemingly heralded the end of the lighthouse, and certainly at some point in the future there will be no more manned lighthouses anywhere in the world. Modern technology will remove the need for anything more than an annual visit, or even less than that. However, lighthouses themselves will remain working long after their keepers have left. Imagine if the GPS satellite failed, or if it was destroyed by an asteroid or a weapon. Consider what would happen if the power on board a ship failed and all the electronic systems shut down. What would sailors rely on then, other than making contact with the nearest place on land, which is so often, of course, a lighthouse. Lighthouses will still be standing there, sailors will still know how to navigate and we will all thank our lucky stars that, with the advent of the new, the old was not completely swept away.

In Greek mythology, the sea nymph Scylla was a sea monster that drowned sailors in the Straits of Messina. Charybdis was a ship-devouring monster that lay in wait opposite Scylla, and mariners had to struggle to pass between these dangers to reach safety on the other side. It comes as no surprise, therefore, that centuries ago beacons were lit on the south-west coast of Italy and the north-east coast of Sicily to help ships negotiate the straits successfully. This tale is symbolic of the journey of the soul, travelling through darkness and difficulty to find light and hope rather than destroying itself upon the rocks. The lighthouse has always been a symbol of what man strives to achieve, both in his interior world and in his physical one.

Lighthouses are inspirational buildings not only in their designs, the feats of engineering involved in physically building them and the emotions they engender, but also in the creativity they arouse in other human endeavours. Artists, writers, poets, film makers and song-smiths have often found themselves drawn to using lighthouses in their work, sometimes symbolically and sometimes literally. Like the travellers who used them as homing beacons, artists the world over have come back time and again to lighthouses as a source of inspiration and beauty.

Lighthouses have featured in countless films, contributing to a sinister or secure atmosphere, simply through their presence. Who can forget the Gay Head lighthouse at Martha's Vineyard, Massachusetts, seen in *Jaws* (1975), or the 1979 film *The Fog*, shot at Point Reyes light, north-west of San Francisco? *Final Analysis* (1992) used Pigeon Point light in California, and *Snow Falling on Cedars* (1999) featured Portland Head light in Maine.

Many artists have been attracted to lighthouses. William Turner and Edward Hopper both famously painted them, and more recently, in 1998, Tacita Dean's 16 mm film *Disappearance at Sea* was short-listed for the Turner prize. Inspired by the loss at sea of the yachtsman Donald Crowhurst, it showed the revolving light of St Abb's Head in Scotland during the course of several hours as the sun sets and the night falls. Lighthouses also present particularly challenging and interesting subjects for still photography. Many photographers – professional and amateur – have travelled considerable distances and gone to great lengths to capture the visual delights of lighthouses and their settings all over the world.

Virginia Woolf spent much of her childhood at Talland House in north Cornwall, from the windows of which she could see a lighthouse perched on the little rocky island

A revolving lighthouse, Sweden.

of Godrevy, 3 miles north of St Ives. Home to a variety of seabirds and waders, the island is grassy on the landward side and the spring brings patches of heather and primroses to adorn it. Built by James Walker in 1859, the white octagonal tower gives warning of a dangerous reef nearby. The Godrevy light was the inspiration for Woolf's novel *To the Lighthouse*, which despite being set in the Hebrides, is actually more descriptive of Cornwall.

Art can only be said to have had a benevolent influence on lighthouses. In 1988, the BBC filmed *The Life and Loves of a She Devil* at Belle Tout lighthouse at Beachy Head in Sussex, restoring the building and replacing the lantern in order to do so. In 1999 the whole building had to be moved about 50 feet back from the unstable cliff edge, and it is now a privately owned bed and breakfast establishment.

Above: Happisburgh, Norfolk.

Opposite (top): Belle Tout, East Sussex.

Opposite (bottom): St Abb's Head, Scotland.

Ever since humankind first ventured out to sea,

people have relied upon visual aids to find their way. As well as natural markers such as the stars, humans have found and created others in the local environment to help identify their position in relation to the world around them. Without doubt, those early sailors who were bold enough to sail in the dark must have been deeply thankful for the fires lit upon cliff top, headland and beach, enabling them to come safely home.

It is not known who first discovered that a high structure could maximize the long-distance visibility of a fire, but there is plenty of evidence that the ancient Egyptians, Greeks and Romans all built and used light towers as navigational tools, and that their empires achieved extra wealth and power because of them. The Colossus at Rhodes, at the entrance to the Greek island's main harbour, is known to have been a landmark, or rather seamark, for ships. It is reputed to have been a 100-foot high bronze figure of Apollo holding a torch. Supposedly, the torch was lit at night to guide ships into harbour. Whether or not this is an accurate description hardly matters – the fact is that it was a man-made visual aid for sailors. It was built around 300 BC and stood for 80 years until an earthquake brought it tumbling down.

The first lighthouse that we can be sure existed is still the most famous: the well-documented Pharos of Alexandria. Commissioned by Ptolemy II, the architect, Sostratus of Gnidus, began work in 261 BC. Nineteen years later, a long time by today's standards, this extraordinary structure, 450 feet high and resting on a base 100 feet square, was completed. If the weather was fine, the open fire at its summit could be seen for nearly 30 miles, and it was known (as was the Colossus), as one of the seven wonders of the ancient world. Logically, one has to assume that such an enormous and expensive

Cape Hatteras, North Carolina.

HISTORY

project was the culmination of knowledge and experience gained from building earlier lighthouses, as it would not have been built if sea lights had not been so highly valued.

Evidently, Sostratus felt that he had achieved an extraordinary feat, as he inscribed his name upon the tower wall. Nervous of his master, he then covered up his inscription and carved Ptolemy's name on top, knowing that in due course the coating would crumble away, leaving his own name to be remembered down the ages. Around 250 years later in AD 113, the Roman writer Pliny expressed his admiration for Ptolemy's generosity of spirit for having permitted Sostratus to engrave his own name. The Pharos lighthouse was named after the island upon which it was built, and it became the most famous lighthouse in the world, being both the largest and the longest serving. In the 13th century it was damaged by an earthquake, but its ruins could still be seen in 1350. The word 'pharos' can be traced in many languages the world over, and lighthouse engineering is still called pharology.

Sostratus was not primitive in his methods of construction: he fused the blocks of stone together with melted lead – a technique that was used some 2,000 years later during the building of the second Eddystone lighthouse at Plymouth. Pliny also referred to other light beacons at Ravenna and Pozzuoli, and images of beacons and lighthouses are frequently found on coins, medals, vases and sarcophagi. Emperor Commodus had a medal struck showing a military expedition leaving the man-made port of Ostia that also depicted its lighthouse, built by the Emperor Claudius.

The Roman Empire was keenly aware of the benefits of lighthouses. The empire was keen to trade, and saw both making huge improvements to existing ports and building artificial ports as worthwhile investments. Ostia became one of the greatest ports, capable of accepting convoys of merchant ships carrying both practical and exotic items from around the world to feed the appetite of Rome. The Romans built many lighthouses around their empire, including the Tour d'Ordre at Boulogne, built by the infamous Emperor Caligula to commemorate his 'victory' over Neptune, the god of the sea. Caligula died before he was 30 years old, but his lighthouse outlasted the Roman Empire, guiding ships for nearly 1,600 years before crashing down in 1644.

Rome's most famous lighthouse legacy, however, is the light at La Coruña on the Galician coast of Spain. Now known as the Tower of Hercules, it was supposedly built during the 2nd century AD. Repaired and rebuilt century after century, La Coruña is the longest-serving lighthouse in the world and, thanks to a particularly good reconstruction in 1791, the structure remains true to the style of the original building.

After the fall of the Roman Empire in the late 5th century AD, much of Europe was plunged into chaos. Trading collapsed and many Roman lighthouses were left to disintegrate, or were attacked and destroyed by barbarians and raiders. Maritime industry dramatically declined, as did ship building, and the lights that brave souls still sailing at night could see were likely to be manned by pirates and smugglers – a tradition that, certainly in England, continued into the 19th century.

The next few hundred years were not kind to the lighthouses of Europe, although the Holy Roman Emperor Charlemagne restored the Tour d'Ordre at Boulogne (it had collapsed in 664), and his son is reputed to have built the first light tower on Cordouan, an island near the mouth of the Gironde River in France. This light tower was rebuilt many times over the centuries and, like La Coruña, still exists today.

As Europe lived through the Dark Ages, other civilizations were striding ahead. In China, for example, tall pagodas were being erected at the entrances to important harbours. The five-storey pagoda built by Buddhist monks at the entrance to Shanghai Harbour is one of the most important national treasures of China, and a pair of pagodas built in the 10th century at Wenzhou Harbour still act as beacons.

The Crusades played a large part in revitalizing the lighthouses of Europe. As soon as it became clear that there would be a steady flow of shipping heading east, traders and businessmen realized that there was money to be made in lighthouses. The various Italian republics began improving their harbours in exchange for trade concessions, and Messina, on the north-east coast of Sicily, became an important Crusader port by the late 12th century, seeing ships safely through the narrow waters that separate Sicily from Italy on their way to the Holy Land. In the 14th century both Venice and Genoa built lighthouses, and by the 15th century fleets from Florence were regularly sailing as far as Beirut, using lighthouses to point the way.

In England at this time, the Church took a hand in the keeping of lights for sailors, and many coastal chapels and monasteries kept beacons lit. When the dissolution of the monasteries began in 1536, King Henry VIII realized something would have to be done to protect trade ships, so he granted a charter to the Guild of the Blessed Trinity to build two permanent towers around the mouth of the River Tyne. The guild was allowed to levy a charge on passing ships in order to fund the maintenance of the towers. During this period, various local seafarers guilds sprang up in Britain's ports and were collectively known as Trinity Houses. Originally set up to care for sailors and their families who found themselves in dire straits, they soon became involved in the building and operation of

The Tower of Hercules, La Coruña, Spain.

lighthouses, and indeed their location. The London Trinity House guild eventually won a royal commission to build and operate lighthouses in England, Wales and the Channel Islands.

In 1556, Queen Elizabeth I passed an act giving Trinity House the authority to build its own beacons. The act also made the removal of any seamark a punishable offence. Trinity House took its time before actually building any lighthouses, however, and it was not until 1609 that the Lowestoft lighthouse in Suffolk was erected. The low-lying Suffolk coast was guarded by a complex mass of shifting sandbanks and lacked significant features by which to find one's way. Year after year, ships bringing coal to London and the south of England from the north-east, as well as other merchant vessels, ran aground, with enormous loss of life. In one terrible storm, over 600 merchant ships were lost. Trinity House was ordered to improve the situation.

Norfolk's coastline was equally treacherous but, in 1617, having been given approval by King James I's Privy Council to build two lighthouses at Winterton in Norfolk, Trinity House met with unexpected resistance from the king himself, and had to accept a ruling by the attorney general that effectively sanctioned privatization. Patents, licenses and leases were granted to various individuals to build and run their own projects and they, too, were able to extract fees from passing ships. This proved to be a profitable business for many and, although fuel costs were high, huge family fortunes were made by those who owned a light on a busy route.

During the English Civil War, the charter of Trinity House was suspended for about 15 years, until King Charles II came to the throne in 1660. The famous diarist Samuel Pepys was involved with Trinity House, only resigning in 1689, and he talked a great deal about this period in his diaries. Pepys despised private lighthouse speculators who were only in it for the money, as opposed to Trinity House who used the income they received for maintenance and new lights and also for the widows and orphans of sailors lost at sea. In 1661, Pepys himself was offered an eighth of all profits if he supported the private application of a lighthouse patent by an individual named Captain Murford.

World trade revived in the 17th century and many technological advances were made. Plymouth became an important town, due to both trade with America and the naval dockyard that was sited there towards the end of the century. Fourteen miles from Plymouth are three dangerous reefs that are almost invisible at high tide. The water is wild around these reefs and is particularly so around the middle rock, known as the Eddystone. In the late 17th century, Trinity House received a lease from the Crown to put a light on the Eddystone to try to halt the terrible toll of ships and sailors that were being lost. The building of the first Eddystone lighthouse was a significant development in lighthouse technology. It was the first in the world to be built away from land, on an isolated rock surrounded by the sea.

Lighthouse design and engineering continued to thrive during the 18th century. As the British Empire expanded, so did the need for good navigational aids, leading to an increase in the number and efficiency of lighthouses the world over. They were still largely lit with open fires, using different types of fuel: candles, wood, oil and coal. North America's first lighthouse was built at Boston in 1716, and the French built one at their fortress on Cape Breton Island, Nova Scotia, in 1734. Lights were also established in China, Japan and India. However, it was the English designer John Smeaton whose techniques, perfected in the middle of the century, were to become the bench-mark for lighthouse engineers throughout the next 200 years.

During the 18th century, it became clear that lighthouses could do more than warn ships to steer clear of dangerous rocks or tricky headlands – they could actually be identifiable, and so provide an accurate navigational aid by which sailors could find their way. In order to be instantly recognizable, some lighthouses showed more than one light, with separate towers built in order to achieve this. Then came the idea of using several lights to lead a ship through the deepest water in a channel. The Scandinavians were adept at this, using coded flashes as a form of identification, and Carlsten in Sweden is the site of the world's first revolving light.

The French physicist Augustin Jean Fresnel made the next leap forward when he invented the dioptric lens in the early 19th century, the first of which was used in the Cordouan lighthouse in France in 1823. The next significant breakthrough came 80 years later, when British inventor Arthur Kitson developed a new type of burner that produced three times as much light using the same amount of fuel. In 1921, another Briton, David Hood, converted the Kitson burner to use petroleum vapour, and this is still sometimes used today when no electricity is available.

Changes in lighthouse location and management were also taking place during the 18th and 19th centuries. At the beginning of the 18th century, most of the existing lights in England were situated on the east coast. However, as the Industrial Revolution vastly increased trade to the west, both Bristol and Liverpool became major seaports, dealing with trade to and from the West Indies and America. Important lighthouses soon began to appear on Britain's west coast. An act of parliament in 1786 set up the

Cordouan, France.

Commissioners of Northern Lighthouses in Edinburgh, and the Commissioners of Irish Lights were also born that year, though it was to be another 80 or so years before they were known by that name (which they still keep today).

In 1789 the federal government in the United States took over responsibility for all 12 existing lighthouses. George Washington was keenly interested in lighthouses, and one of his first actions as president was to write to the keeper of Sandy Hook lighthouse, asking him to keep his light burning until Congress could provide funds for its maintenance. Thomas Jefferson was also keen on lighthouses, and as interest in them increased, so did the number of lighthouses, which grew to 325 by 1852. That year, the federal government set up the Lighthouse Board, based on existing European models, and the situation continued thus until the US Coast Guard took over responsibility in 1939. They now maintain about 100,000 lights of various descriptions, of which around 1,000 are actual lighthouses. Today, many of these are supported by groups of local enthusiasts, and largely fund themselves through tourism.

Similar changes also occurred in Canada. After the first lighthouse was built by the French at Cape Breton Island, Nova Scotia, the British built another, near the entrance to Halifax Harbour. Although decades passed before more were erected, a great many were built during the 19th century. Electrification occurred early in the 20th century and automation began in the 1940s. When it announced that many of its smaller structures were no longer necessary, the government was taken by surprise by the strength of feeling expressed by local populations. While there are only a few manned lighthouses remaining in Canada, government policy is now to help local preservation groups take ownership of local lights.

Although China used lights in pagodas and beacons to aid sailors, it was not until 1868, when Sir Robert Hart set up a Marine Customs Department in China, that lighthouses really began to proliferate there. Sir Robert persuaded the Chinese to allow him to establish lights on the most dangerous parts of the Chinese coastline that bordered shipping channels linking the world. Starting with buoys and lightships, Hart soon organized for lighthouses to be prefabricated in England and shipped over to China. Meanwhile, the Japanese approached the Stevenson family to build their first lighthouse, which was also prefabricated in England. The Japanese then made copies of this lighthouse and set them all around their coastline.

The Stevenson family made its name as Scottish lighthouse engineers who, for over 100 years in the 18th and 19th centuries, dominated the Northern Lighthouse Board. Robert Stevenson decided that it would be possible to build a lighthouse similar to the one at Eddystone at Bell Rock, a notoriously dangerous sunken ledge at the entrance to the Firth of Forth. Having achieved this, Robert went on to build 17 other lighthouses around Scotland, and his three sons, David, Thomas and Alan, built many more. Alan Stevenson was particularly well known for his expertise in optics, having studied the remarkable young French engineer Augustin Jean Fresnel's lenses in Paris in the 1830s. He designed and built the Skerryvore lighthouse and persuaded the Northern Lighthouse Board to use a Fresnel lens for the light. Stevenson improved on the original Fresnel design, and before long these lenses had spread across the whole of the British Empire.

In 1859, Trinity House became the first lighthouse authority to use electricity in the South Foreland light and, just a few years later, the French put their first arc lamp into

Cape Heve lighthouse. This use of electricity transformed the job of lighthouse keeper from that of an unskilled labourer to a highly skilled technician.

In 1886, the Lighthouse Board of the United States set an electric light into the Statue of Liberty's torch, where it acted as a beacon in New York's harbour for 15 years. By the turn of the 20th century, work was underway to electrify all lighthouses and, in 1910, Congress established the US Lighthouse Service to take over where the existing Lighthouse Board left off. George Putnam was named the first commissioner of lighthouses, by which time there were more than 10,000 lights of varying descriptions to be maintained. Putnam was in charge for 25 years and oversaw the installation of many new developments, such as the Canadian invention of the diaphone, a compressed air foghorn. This was invented by JP Northery Ltd of Toronto in 1902 to resolve persistent problems with fog in the essential St Lawrence Seaway, where the cold Arctic current meets the warmth of the Gulf Stream. Two-tone fog signals came about in 1915, and the automated replacement of blown bulbs arrived the following year. The navy took over the servicing of lighthouses for the duration of US involvement in World War I, but returned it to Putnam as soon as they were able.

The 1920s and 1930s brought much in the way of new automation, including telephones, automatic timers and, by 1934, a remote control radio system that enabled the operation of unmanned lights. In retrospect, these developments heralded today's fully automated lights and were therefore the death knell of the lighthouse keeper – epitomized by the automation in 1999 of North America's oldest beacon, the Boston Harbor light.

Above: The Statue of Liberty, New York.

Right: A pile lighthouse at Key Largo, Florida.

Other related developments include the use of lightships in the 19th century. These are still used today, as are fully automated floating lights or buoys. Until the 1980s, lightships were manned, but because they were also moored, they were sometimes hit by ships unable to see them in fog. They, too, are now unmanned.

During the 19th century, another type of lighthouse construction was conceived: pile lighthouses. These were towers built on wrought-iron legs, which lessened the pressure of the waves by allowing the water to swirl around and through them. Unfortunately, most of the early pile lighthouses were short lived – many were sunk into sand, which the sea washed away until the structures collapsed. However, over time, it became clear that they were a sensible system for use in coastal waters if not out at sea, and indeed the chain of lighthouses along the Florida Keys are constructed in this way. In 1907, a pile lighthouse was built in the Malacca Straits, lighting the way for the vast amount of shipping travelling to and from Singapore. Alexander Mitchell, from Belfast, invented the screw pile, which could be screwed into coral or mud and was a vast improvement on the early pile lighthouses, and Singapore-based engineers drew on this to develop their own system.

Of course, it was not just lighthouse design and construction that altered over the years – the methods of lighting also changed, from the ancient days of open fires, through to later use of oil and gas, and then the arrival of electricity in the 1920s. Nowadays, most land-based lighthouses are supplied with electricity from the national grid, but those that are sited offshore either have their own generator or use solar and wind power to charge up batteries to activate the lights and keep the systems going.

Nuclear energy never really got off the ground for use in lighthouses – the only one that exists is a thermonuclear generator that was installed in Rathlin O'Birne lighthouse in north-west Ireland. The AGA company, founded in Sweden at the beginning of the 20th century and now renowned for its cookers/heaters, originally worked on improved light systems for lighthouses. They designed the lights at Rathlin O'Birne, using low-voltage halogen bulbs powered by batteries charged by a nuclear generator. By the 1920s, AGA automatic lighthouses had been sited all over the world, in places such as the southern edge of South America, the Arctic Circle and Africa – places so remote that they had previously been impossible to light.

Currently, most lighthouses are either maintained by occasional visiting technicians or use a shore-based computerized and centralized control system that allows the operator to spot anything going wrong and to correct it instantly. Another modern change to both existing lighthouses and any new light towers that may be built in the future is the inclusion of a helipad. This feature, together with new technology, means that remote lighthouses no longer need to be serviced via the sea and can be reached by helicopter and maintained on an annual or even biennial basis.

Future lighthouses may simply be a super strong light contained in a narrow pillar that supports a landing pad at the top. The day of the lighthouse keeper is all but over, thanks to automation, and the global positioning system, a relatively inexpensive item that anyone can buy to pinpoint where in the world they are, using signals from satellites. Old-style lighthouses are expensive to maintain and, as there is no real need for them any more, lighthouse fees are no longer paid by trade vessels. As a result, traditional

lighthouses the world over need to raise money from other sources to keep going. This is why so many are being converted to museums or used as guesthouse accommodation. Peggy's Cove in Nova Scotia, for example, is still a working lighthouse, but during the tourist season it operates as a post office. An ex-lighthouse in Harlingen, Holland, meanwhile, has been transformed into beautifully appointed holiday apartments. Even Gibbs Hill light in Bermuda, one of the oldest cast-iron lighthouses in the world, has had to move with the times. Built in 1846 to warn ships of the treacherous reefs just to the west of Bermuda, it is 117 feet high and visible from 40 miles away. Since 1964, when it was automated, its keeper's dwelling has contained a tearoom and a gift shop like countless other lighthouses around the world.

The primary function of lighthouses is not, however, under threat while there are still great stretches of difficult coastline around the world that need illuminating. Even now, new lighthouses are sometimes built. In the late 1980s, the Spanish decided that they needed a new lighthouse on the Costa Dorada, so it was agreed that a competition should be held to determine the best design. Ample time was factored in to allow for responses from various interested parties, such as environmentalists, the tourism authority and local groups concerned with its impact on their day-to-day lives. Finally, a structure was built and the official lighting-up ceremony was held on the stroke of the year 2000. In 1998, the Japanese inaugurated their own new lighthouse at Takamatsu, on the north-east coast of Shikoku, using an aluminium frame and glass bricks that are lit up at night for extra visual impact. This marvellous light enables vessels to find their way more easily through the channel that separates the main island of Honshu from Shikoku, one of its smaller neighbours.

Top: **Gibb's Hill, Bermuda.**

Bottom: **Peggy's Cove, Nova Scotia, Canada.**

The very first lighthouse to be built in North

America was the Boston Harbor light in 1716, situated on Little Brewster Island near the harbour's entrance. The light at the top of the 70-foot tall stone tower was first produced by candles and then by lamps burning whale oil. During the American Revolution, retreating British troops blew up and destroyed the Boston Harbor light, which was not replaced until 1783, when the British accepted defeat and granted American independence. Curiously, the British also blew up the first lighthouse built in Canada.

Boston Harbor light is not, however, the oldest continuously working lighthouse in North America – that accolade goes to the Sandy Hook lighthouse at New Jersey, built in 1764 and still going strong today.

The colony of Massachusetts built the Boston Harbor light at the urging of the owners of New England's merchant ships and other businessmen, and all ships coming into harbour were charged a levy of one penny per ton, and another penny on leaving. Coasters had to pay two shillings each on leaving, while fishing vessels paid five shillings per year. This paid for the upkeep of the building and also lighthouse keeper George Worthylake's small salary.

Today, visitors can see a list of the names of more than 60 lighthouse keepers who looked after Boston Harbor light for the best part of 300 years, until it became fully automated in 1999. Unfortunately, the first two keepers both quickly came to grief. George Worthylake, who was also a shepherd, lasted for two years, during which time his salary of £50 per annum was increased to £70 because his light-tending duties had prevented him from being able to save 59 of his sheep from drowning during a bad storm. This devotion to his light was due in no small part to his contract of employment, which obliged him to keep the light burning from sunset to sunrise or face a fine of £100.

Boston Harbor, Massachusetts.

NORTH AMERICA

Sadly, Worthylake, his wife, daughter and negro slave were all drowned when their boat capsized while returning from a trip to nearby Noddle's Island. The second keeper, Robert Saunders, was also unlucky – he drowned in a similar accident only weeks after taking up his post.

The Boston Harbor light has yet another claim to fame: it was the recipient of the first North American fog signal. This took the form of a cannon that was sited at the bottom of the tower and fired in response to ships' cannons, which fired as they tried to enter the fog-bound harbour. In 1788, five years after a replacement tower was built, it was equipped with a lightning conductor (made by Benjamin Franklin) because this unlucky tower was receiving a great many lightning strikes. This outraged the religious right-wingers of the day, who said that human beings should not try to prevent God from doing what he so obviously willed and that it was deeply sinful to try to interfere. They did not win this particular battle.

Meanwhile, in Georgia, Colonel James Oglethorpe, who had founded the colony, decided that his supply ships needed help to find Savannah, which lies about 20 miles upriver from the low-lying coast. In 1736, a 90-foot high wooden tower was built. It was intended as a daymark and had no light. However, about five years later it collapsed during a storm and the tower that was quickly put up to replace it presumably did have a light, as this time the tower had a roof. The tower lasted about 30 years, when it was replaced by a much hardier brick structure.

Three or four more lighthouses were built during the 1740s and 1750s, and then in 1761 the authorities in New York held a lottery in order to fund the building of a lighthouse in the harbour. This lottery only generated a paltry £26, but refusing to give up, the authorities organized another lottery the following year. This time the venture was much more successful and enough money was raised to fund an octagonal tower with a 7-foot high lantern housing with a copper roof. The whole structure stood 103 feet tall and was built by Isaac Conro. The original tower, still standing today, is called the Sandy Hook lighthouse, and it is the oldest continuously working lighthouse in the United States.

In 1789, after the American Revolution, Congress passed a bill that took responsibility for building lighthouses away from the individual colonies and gave it instead to Alexander Hamilton, the first secretary to the Treasury. To begin with, he ran the system on a day-to-day basis, looking after the 12 existing lighthouses and sending new contracts to President George Washington to be signed. However, after three years he passed responsibility to the commissioner for revenue. President Washington was a great fan of lighthouses, as he believed in the importance of commerce. He was known to make notes of likely sites for navigational aids on his travels and, in 1756 at the age of 25, he visited Montauk Point on a tour of Long Island and told his companions that he thought it was a perfect spot for a lighthouse. Little could he have imagined that 40 years later, close to the end of his presidency, work would be starting on the Montauk Point light, and that it would be built right there where he had stood.

After an initial reluctance on the part of Congress to put their hands deep into their pockets on behalf of lighthouse construction, they came around to the idea and soon several splendid new towers were built. However, it was not until the 1850s that US lighthouse technology began to catch up with Europe. Until then, there had been no national standard of construction: many lighthouses were flimsily built and the optics were often secondhand imports from European lighthouses that had been upgraded with

Above: Tybee Island, Georgia.　Opposite: Sandy Hook lighthouse, New Jersey.

new Fresnel lenses from Paris. This reluctance to invest in lighthouses was largely due to one man – Stephen Pleasanton – who began life as a book-keeper and never lost his loyalty to his original job.

In 1820 Stephen Pleasanton was an auditor in the United States Treasury when his office took over the business of the nation's maritime lights. Although during his 30-year tenure the number of lighthouses and lightships increased from about 70 to approximately 370, Stephen Pleasanton was always more interested in keeping down costs than in building an efficient system.

Pleasanton fell under the influence of a ship's captain-turned-inventor named Winslow Lewis. Lewis invented a lamp and reflector system, using a design that had already been dropped by the Stevenson family in Scotland (the Stevensons dominated the Northern Lighthouse Board of Scotland for generations and were extremely influential around the world). Lewis persuaded Pleasanton that his lamp would be effective, both in terms of use and cost and, consequently, the government decided to use his system in all lighthouses – regardless of the fact that neither the mirror nor the lens was efficient.

Flush with his success, Lewis went on to bid for contracts to construct light towers. As his bids were always unrealistically low, he was frequently successful. Although some of his towers were solid, most of them either collapsed spontaneously or were blown down in storms after only a few years of service. Despite the many seamen who pleaded with Pleasanton to listen to sense, he refused to do so, even after ships came to grief yards from lighthouses with lights so dim that they simply could not be seen at all.

The new Fresnel lenses were expensive – thousands of dollars apiece – and Pleasanton could not bear spending money. At that time the United States was not the immensely rich country it is today (the economy was still largely based on agriculture), but Congress itself eventually ordered Pleasanton to try out the new lenses. A couple of large lenses were put into a lighthouse on Nantucket Island, and a couple of smaller ones elsewhere. These were greeted enthusiastically by sailors, who described them as 'blazing stars' and gave them other lyrical names. Pleasanton was not convinced, however, and ensured that these comments were not passed on. In the end it took another lighthouse disaster to see Pleasanton removed from his position in 1852 – 32 years after first taking up the post.

Between 1832 and 1841, at least 40 ships had been wrecked in the area of Minot's Ledge at the edge of Boston Bay, and a lighthouse for the ledge was soon in the process of being built. Winslow Lewis's nephew Isaiah persuaded the authorities that it would be possible to build a new design of lighthouse directly over the ledge. It would be a lodging and lantern set high up on eight cast-iron legs. This would allow the wind and the waves to pass through the structure without causing any damage. It was an extremely arduous project on which to work and was completed too late for some people – in October 1849, a ship named *Saint John*, packed to the gunnels with Irish immigrants, hit the ledge. The ship broke into pieces and bodies were washed up on nearby beaches for days.

To build the lighthouse, the rock first had to be drilled with deep holes into which the iron legs could be hammered. This work could only be done during a short period each day when the tide was out and the ledge was above water. On New Year's Day 1850, three years after construction began, the light was finally lit.

Above: **St Joseph, Michigan.**

Right: **A Fresnel lens.**

Although sailors were delighted with the new light, the keepers reported that the tower swayed and felt unstable during bad weather. The head keeper resigned, fearing for his life, while his replacement was told that the movement was normal. In March 1851, barely one year after completion, the tower gave way during a bad storm and two assistant keepers perished with it. Both keepers were found; one had drowned and washed up on the shore, while the other was discovered still alive on a reef, but died soon afterwards from exposure. A temporary lightship was placed at the reef almost immediately, and a more permanent one was installed there in 1855, where it remained for the five years that it took to build the 114-foot high, solid granite replacement tower.

The uproar caused by this latest disaster forced Congress to appoint a commission called the Lighthouse Board to investigate all existing navigational lights. The board's report was damning: many lighthouses were crumbling, the lights themselves were useless, the keepers were being housed in dreadful conditions and the US lighthouse service was far behind those of Britain and Europe. Stephen Pleasanton left his post and the Lighthouse Board was given total responsibility for all US navigational aids and tasked with bringing them up to scratch. The Lighthouse Board was quickly able to get better funding from Congress and, by the end of the decade, not only had Fresnel lenses been placed in most lighthouses, but also sufficient resources were available for American research into optics. In 1860, after five years of complicated and arduous work, the second Minot's Ledge lighthouse was lit. It remains alight today, although it was fully automated in 1947.

The new authority made many changes in the organization of lighthouses, insisting that keepers and crew wore uniforms and kept both lighthouses and dwellings in perfect condition. Inspectors made unannounced spot checks and sacked personnel if they failed to meet the expected standard. They also brought in innovative engineers from the army, such as George Meade. Meade was intrigued by the cast-iron eight-legged structure that had been the first Minot's Ledge lighthouse, and came up with a revised design that resulted in a series of towers along the Florida Keys, fixed into the reefs with screw piles. Of these, Carysfort Reef, Sand Key and Sombrero Key, screw-pile towers built in the 1850s, are still operational.

At the same time, the Lighthouse Board also decided to do something about the United States' west coast – as yet virtually untouched by navigational aids. They employed a civilian engineer named Francis Gibbons to build eight lighthouses scattered along 1,000 miles of coastline. In 1853, his first lighthouse was completed on Alcatraz Island in San Francisco Bay. This was made to look like an east coast house built around a brick tower, and was followed by several more in the same vein elsewhere. The Alcatraz lighthouse lasted until 1906, when it collapsed during the famous San Francisco earthquake that devastated the city. In 1909, a reinforced concrete tower replaced it. Most tourists go to look at the new lighthouse at the same time as they visit the now defunct prison. However, the tower and the lens are all that is left: the keeper's residence was destroyed in 1970 by Native American political activists occupying the island.

The Victorian work ethic and the technological advances of the Industrial Revolution that took hold of Britain during the late 19th century were also embraced by Americans and the Lighthouse Board gradually expanded its area of operations up and down the west coast of the United States from Alaska to Hawaii, both onshore and on remote rocks and ledges surrounded by the Pacific Ocean.

Sombrero Key, Florida.

In 1872, it decided to build a much-needed lighthouse at Race Rock, near the north-east end of Long Island Sound. The rock owes its name to the speed with which the tides and 6-mile-per-hour current sweep over and through the deadly reef that lies just beneath the water. At its highest point, the reef is no more than 3 feet below the surface of the water, which, when combined with thick fog and ice, made building a light here a priority. During the 1860s, many ships – including eight large ones – went down on this reef. F Hopkinson Smith, who also designed the foundations for the Statue of Liberty, was given the job of chief engineer with Captain Thomas Scott, another engineer, as his second-in-command. The terrifying conditions and the fact that the nearest supply point was 8 miles away, made their job appear to be almost impossible. Developing an imaginative plan, however, F Hopkinson Smith raised the level of the reef to well above sea level by sinking thousands of rocks. Huge lumps of rock, some weighing as much as 7 tons, were brought by barge and dropped onto the reef. This work continued for a year or more, and finally at low tide it was possible to see the 60-foot diameter island that had been formed.

The next step was to level this artificial island in order to build upon it. This was an amazing feat. Each rock had several holes drilled very carefully into it and just the right amount of explosive placed in each hole. The workers used extra long fuses so that they had time to scramble into their boat and let the tide whisk them away to a safe distance before the explosion occurred. This work was so precise that the explosions left a flat surface. The men then had to row back to the island, sometimes against the current, which required an enormous amount of time and energy from each worker. To save on labour and time, Captain Scott had the idea of using explosive to make a deep hole in the middle of the island, and putting a roof over it in order to provide a shelter for his workers. It must have been hellish operating in these conditions, as the hole was constantly half full of water and at high tide the workers were submerged up to their necks.

Progress was slow and various disasters hampered the work, but their worst came with the realization that the stones at the bottom of this artificial island were gradually sliding down a slope on the seabed itself. Doughty Captain Scott went down himself to see exactly what could be done to remedy the situation. He realized that they would have to undo all their work and move all those huge rocks that had been heaved into the water. His new plan involved setting the rocks in a circle, like a breakwater, and then blasting a way down through the middle of the circle to the sand at the bottom to uncover the rock beneath. They would then fill this hole with a vast amount of concrete to take it up to low-tide level and put a granite foundation for the lighthouse on top.

Four large derricks were organized and moved out to surround the rock. They were chained down and connected to each other by thick wire ropes. Siting the derricks took three weeks with 20 men working at a time. Twice they crashed over, but extraordinarily, no one was hurt. Captain Scott supervised the divers, who had the unenviable task of moving each boulder to its new position using chains and slings. Finally, they managed to build a stone wall that stood 8 inches higher than the water level at low tide.

They then began to work on the inside of the wall, putting in place, one at a time, circular iron bands, 60 feet in diameter and 3 feet deep, and then filling them with concrete. Each iron band was slightly smaller in diameter than the one beneath it, and eventually a solid platform rose above the water. This process took five years, 10,000 tons of rocks and $250,000 to achieve – a truly phenomenal feat. A huge conical pier, made of granite and standing 30 feet high, was then built as a base for the lighthouse itself. This took another three years and another $30,000. Finally, after almost eight years, a square, granite, two-storey keeper's house with the tower rising up from the centre was ready, and the light was lit on New Year's Day in 1879. Race Rock still flashes its red and white warning lights, which can be seen from 14 miles away. Until 1978 when it was automated, keepers lived there all the time.

Fourteen Foot Bank is another example of this method of lighthouse building, known as a caisson foundation. Fourteen Foot Bank stands around 4 miles from the shore in Delaware Bay. It is an enormous shoal, 1,300 feet wide and 6,000 feet long, and it is as shallow as its name suggests. A lightship had been sited there from 1876, but had to be moved to safety each winter because of the dangers of floating ice. Of course, winter was the time when a light was most needed, so the Lighthouse Board decided to build a tower on a concrete-filled caisson made of cast iron. As there had been a recent, expensive disaster on Rothersand Shoal when trying to sink a caisson, the Lighthouse Board took their time in deciding the best way to make one on Fourteen Foot Bank. In 1883, however, they accepted the plans of their chief engineer, Major Heap, and gave him the go-ahead to start work.

Major Heap planned to build and sink a huge cylinder made of cast iron at the site. It was to be 73 feet high and 35 feet in diameter. The government agreed to supply the materials and put out tenders for building it. A civil engineering company from New York won the contract, but had to agree to deposit a large sum of money with the government

A caisson foundation lighthouse, Harbor of Refuge, Delaware.

as insurance. They began with a wooden box, 40 feet square, solid at the top and open at the bottom, with all the joints made waterproof. A circular airshaft descended from the roof to the ground. The 18-foot high caisson was then built on the roof and around the airshaft, and concrete was poured between the airshaft and the walls of the cylinder. They then began to sink both the box and the caisson into the sand by letting in water through valves. All went well until the structure touched the bottom of the sea, at which point it began to keel over sideways. The top of the caisson was only inches away from the waves, and it seemed likely that the government would keep the insurance money.

Tugs were immediately sent to the shore to pick up the vast amounts of stone and rubble; meanwhile, the engineers made large bags or pockets and placed them inside the top section of the cylinder that was still above the waterline. These were filled with the stones that had been brought back from the shore and, little by little, the caisson was brought upright again. Then they pumped the water out of the caisson as fast as they could and replaced it with concrete, which ensured that the sharp edge of the outer wooden box dug itself right down into the sand. The structure was now utterly firm, but the cylinder needed to be built up higher because it was still far too close to the surface of the sea. More sections of the cylinder were bolted on until it reached 20 feet above sea level.

Inside the wooden caisson box, three gangs of eight men worked eight-hour shifts wearing hats fitted with candle holders in which burned ordinary candles. As the sand was dug away, the cylinder was filled with concrete. After digging and concreting for a month, they had reached their target depth of 33 feet. The working space was then packed with sand and the airshaft filled with concrete. Other workers were busy tipping

6,000 tons of stones around the base of the cylinder to make it as strong and impervious to the movement of the sea as they could. On top of this circular rock that now rose from the sea was built a rather extraordinary and eccentric three-storey house with a small tower attached to it. The entire project had taken two years to complete and came in well under budget.

The lighthouses at Bass Harbor Head and West Quoddy Head are both typical examples of Maine architecture and, as such, are interesting as more than lighthouses. Bass Harbor Head is a charming little lighthouse, with a white brick tower, black gallery and light, and a white-painted clapboard cottage next door. Built in 1858, a beacon has shone out ever since to guide fishermen in from Blue Hill Bay. Bass Harbor is a well-known centre for lobster fishing and boasts a fleet of gaily painted lobster boats that seems to complement the lighthouse. Nowadays, Blue Hill Bay is a much-loved tourist destination and visitors to the Acadia National Park are allowed to walk around the grounds of the lighthouse, though they cannot go inside as it is still used by the Coast Guard. Automated in 1974, the lighthouse uses its original Fresnel lens, surrounded by red panels outside which produce its red beam. The tower itself is only 32 feet tall, but is sited on a red granite boulder cliff with a fir tree forest as its backdrop, making it one of the prettiest of North America's lighthouses.

The structure at West Quoddy Head, built earlier in 1808, is also rather small at 49 feet tall. It stands near the edge of a 40-foot cliff overlooking the Bay of Fundy, famous for its frighteningly fast tides of up to 70 feet. It is the most easterly point of the United States and was therefore the very first place in America to see the dawning of the new millennium. Built during Thomas Jefferson's presidency, the original tower was demolished in 1858 and replaced with a brick one. Painted in red and white bands with a red, conical hat on top of the black-painted light casing and gallery, it has a white-walled, red-roofed clapboard cottage beside it. It, too, has a Fresnel lens that is still in use and an automated foghorn housed in its own little red-roofed, white-walled brick house. The buildings and the land have now been incorporated into Quoddy Head State Park and the keeper's residence has become the visitors centre.

On the west coast, close to Richmond in California, stands the East Brother lighthouse. Built in 1874 to show ships the way into San Francisco Bay, it stands on a tiny island off San Pablo Point. The 48-foot high clapboard tower appears to be the central part of the surrounding house, but in fact it is a detached structure. In the classic Victorian style of the area, the house has a lovely exterior staircase leading up to a partial verandah, and a rather ornate gallery in a matching style that surrounds the light on the tower. During the 1960s, there was a move to demolish this charming building, but local pressure ensured a preservation order. Nowadays, the house is a bed and breakfast establishment, and visitors not only wake up to a fantastic view of the bay but also know that their money is going towards the upkeep of the building.

Biloxi lighthouse in Mississippi could not be more different. Built in 1848, it is a cast-iron tower, 61 feet high and painted white with a black verandah. It is commonly believed to be the oldest cast-iron lighthouse in the southern states of the US, and it has stood proud through dangerous and difficult times such as the Civil War and Hurricane Camille, which demolished much of Biloxi in 1968. It has been owned and operated by the city of Biloxi since the Coast Guard divested itself of it in 1968. Interestingly, for over 60 years, up until 1929, the lighthouse was tended by women – first Maria Younghans and

West Quoddy Head, Maine.

Above: Makapu'u point, Hawaii.

Right: Bass Harbor Head, Maine.

then her daughter Miranda. The Americans were rather less sexist in their attitude to women keepers than Trinity House. The English institution thought it was not a suitable job for a woman – conveniently ignoring the fact that many keepers lived with their families in lighthouses or on lighthouse stations, and their wives and daughters were effectively used as unpaid assistants.

Ida Lewis is another well-known female lighthouse keeper, who took over the Lime Rock lighthouse in Newport, Rhode Island, in 1872 on the death of her father. The Lighthouse Board made her the official keeper in 1879 and she continued there until her late 60s, when she was found dying on the floor of the lantern room. She received many awards for life saving, was written about in magazines and newspapers and met President Ulysses Grant.

Two lighthouses on the Hawaiian Islands in the Pacific Ocean that deserve a mention are Makapu'u Point lighthouse, which stands at the eastern tip of the island of Oahu and guards the approach to Honolulu, and Kalaupapa lighthouse on the Kalaupapa Peninsula of Molokai Island. Makapu'u Point lighthouse was established in 1909 and boasts the most powerful Fresnel lens in the United States. The 46-foot tower stands on a lava cliff that raises the height of the beacon to 420 feet. The guiding light can be seen from 28 miles away and is a familiar sight to the many thousands of ships that sail to the island and its capital city.

Kalaupapa is very different. The lighthouse is set on a peninsula that is separated from the rest of the island of Molokai by high cliffs, and sailors have always found it difficult to find a safe haven on these rocky shores. The 138-foot tower is the highest in Hawaii and is now a part of the Kalaupapa National Historical Park. Visitors can only get there by climbing down the 2,000-foot cliffs, either on foot or by mule. They come to see not only the lighthouse but also the remains of an old leper colony, for which the peninsula was famous. Tales of tragedy still abound on the island, although the colony closed years ago.

Cape Hatteras lighthouse on Bodie Island, North Carolina, is one of the best-known lighthouses in the world. The federal government commissioned the first tower in 1803, but although it stood 90 feet high, it was not tall enough to be of much use. Ships still piled into the shoals that lie to the south of Hatteras Island, not having noticed that a lighthouse was there at all. In due course, as a result of many complaints, it was raised to 150 feet in height, but this was still not enough. More ships foundered there during the Civil War and when the war was over the Lighthouse Board replaced it completely with the existing tower, which was lit in 1870. That, however, was not the end of its troubles – the shoreline suffers badly from erosion, and several times the lighthouse has been threatened by the Atlantic Ocean coming within 200 yards of it. In the 1990s the erosion became severe, with the ocean pushing in around three sides of the tower, despite tons of sand being pumped onto the beach in an effort to secure its safety. Finally, the National Parks Service transported the lighthouse almost 1,000 yards inland and put it on a solid foundation. Visitors come from far and wide to visit Cape Hatteras lighthouse, and it has become symbolic of the efforts that are being made throughout the world to preserve and restore buildings of historic interest.

At the other end of the country, near Haines in Alaska, stands Eldred Rock lighthouse, the oldest lighthouse in Alaska and something of a national treasure. Built in 1905, it is an unusual large octagonal building, painted white with a red roof and a 56-foot high tower in the centre. It was automated in the early 1970s, and is now solar powered. This leaves the building vulnerable as it is no longer necessary, but local people

Eldred Rock, Alaska.

are keen to preserve it, and the Haines Museum would like to own and restore it. The light is still operational, and indeed is still needed as many a ship has foundered there.

Another lighthouse that has had a narrow escape thanks to the local citizenry is the Holland Harbor light in Michigan. The Coast Guard wished to lose this lighthouse during the 1970s, but fortunately were pushed into giving it a reprieve. They now maintain the light itself, while the local historical commission own and maintain the building. It is not surprising that the lighthouse is held in such affection by sailors and residents alike: standing on a pier at the entrance to Holland Harbor, the lighthouse is painted a vivid bright red, hence its nickname 'Big Red'.

Canada is one of the largest countries in the

world and boasts a coastline of about 150,000 miles. With the Pacific on its west coast, the Atlantic to the east and the Arctic way up north, it also has four of the Great Lakes – Superior, Huron, Erie and Ontario – as well as thousands of other navigable lakes and rivers. In addition, it has thousands of islands – from the vast Newfoundland to the east and Vancouver to the west, to the small and privately owned, or even the tiny and uninhabited. The great city of Montreal itself is, of course, an island, set in the middle of the St Lawrence Seaway. It could safely be said that Canada needed lights.

In the 16th century, a few adventurous Europeans made it to Canada, but it was a Frenchman, Jacques Cartier, who found the St Lawrence River in 1534, and staked France's claim to the whole of the surrounding area. At that time, the native Huron word for a small settlement was 'kanata' and Cartier used the word 'canada' in his diaries to describe the area he had claimed. In due course this word became the name for the whole country.

Samuel de Champlain was another French explorer in the early 17th century. He founded the city of Quebec in 1608 and fortified it in 1620. In 1635, while exploring farther down the St Lawrence River, he came across a small Iroquois village at the foot of a mountain on an island in the river. In 1642 Sieur de Maisonneuve founded a missionary post named Ville Marie there. The mountain was named Mont Royale, and the town that sprang up there, now known as Montreal, was named after it.

The French were mainly interested in the fish and fur trades, and by 1663 Canada was a French province. During the 17th century they pushed out their boundaries to the west and south, down to what is now Louisiana. At the same time, the British, always interested in trading opportunities, began to take an interest in the area. The Hudson Bay Trading Company (still a major Canadian department store chain) moved into Hudson Bay in northern Ontario, and the fur trade became big business.

Gradually the British moved into parts of the Canadian eastern seaboard, dominating most of Nova Scotia and Newfoundland by the early 18th century. In 1745, a British army from New England marched north to begin a war with the French. The end of French domination was heralded by their defeat at Quebec city in 1759, and Canada was formally handed over to the British by the Treaty of Paris in 1763.

The fate of the first lighthouse in Canada was intrinsically tied to this series of events. Built by the French at Louisbourg on Cape Breton Island, Nova Scotia, in 1734, this lighthouse was only the second light to have been built in the whole of North America. The British destroyed it during a siege in 1758 and it was not rebuilt for almost 80 years. The ruins of the original lighthouse can still be seen at the base of the existing Louisbourg lighthouse, which dates from 1924.

The second Canadian lighthouse to be built was on Sambro Island, at the entrance to the harbour at Halifax, Nova Scotia. Lit in 1760, it has been restored and renewed over the centuries, and is the oldest continuously operational lighthouse in North America. The building of this light was followed in 1788 by the construction of Cape Roseway on McNutt's Island. A splendid 92-foot high octagonal tower, clad in clapboard and braced with wooden timbers, it was sadly hit by lightning in 1959, and the subsequent fire damaged it so badly that it was not considered repairable. A replacement tower was built in 1960 and is still operational. In 1791, a lighthouse was built on Partridge Island at the entrance to St John, New Brunswick. There have been three more lighthouses since

Cape Bonavista, Newfoundland.

Above: Peggy's Cove, Nova Scotia.

Left: La Martre lighthouse, Gaspé Peninsula, Quebec.

then on Partridge Island and the last, an octagonal concrete tower, was built in 1959. In these early days of lighthouse building, the designers took their ideas from existing British models. Most were slender, conical towers made of stone or brick.

A Canadian version of Trinity House was established in Lower Canada (today's Quebec) in 1805, and quickly set to work. They built a lighthouse on Ile Verte at the meeting point of the St Lawrence and Saguenay rivers in 1809, which is now the third oldest existing lighthouse in Canada. This was followed with at least seven more, built farther downstream, over the course of the next 30 years.

Trinity House also built the Cape Spear (1836) and Cape Bonavista (1843) lighthouses on Newfoundland, and furnished them with the old reflector lamp systems from Inchkeith and Bell Rock lighthouses in Scotland (both had been upgraded with more modern equipment). By the late 1850s, the Scottish engineer John Brown had completed several more lighthouses of this traditional design in Quebec, Newfoundland and around the Great Lakes. It was becoming clear that Canada needed to improve its navigational aids to prevent economic losses so, after concerted lobbying, the British government agreed to bear the cost of a three-year building programme in Canada. The resulting 'imperial' lights were built of brick or stone, often quarried and shaped by Scottish stonemasons and then shipped to the colony as ballast. Four lighthouses were built along the St Lawrence, six on Lake Huron and a couple on the Pacific Seaboard, off Vancouver Island at Race Rock and Fisgard Island. Cap des Rosiers, built on the Gaspé Peninsula in 1858, is the tallest lighthouse in Canada and is a typical example of an imperial lighthouse.

At this point, however, Canadian designers began developing their own style, and using wood because it was so cheaply and widely available. They started to build the 'pepperpot' type of lighthouse – a square-based pyramid shape, often octagonal, with a square gallery at the top, just under the light. These were practical because, should the channel in which they were located silt up, they were very easy to move. Most of these wooden lighthouses were painted red and white, occasionally with the addition of black and in some cases they were even entirely red. A good example of this is the lighthouse of Riviere La Martre on the Gulf of St Lawrence. Now the site of a museum, it consists of a classic octagonal tower with an unusual circular cast-iron lantern, and all of it, including the keeper's house, is painted a red reminiscent of the Canadian flag, with its maple leaf design. The colour no doubt adds to its visibility in winter, when the ground around it is covered in snow.

Gannet Rock is a black and white lighthouse on Canada's eastern seaboard. Its only spots of colour are the red lantern at the top and the door to the keeper's cottage. This was the last manned lighthouse in eastern Canada, and the visits from the Canadian Coast Guard landing on the helipad in their red and white helicopters must have been joyfully received in later years. Made of wood and sited where it receives the full fury of the Atlantic waves, this lighthouse has survived for over 170 years.

Peggy's Cove in Nova Scotia, built in 1868, is well loved and a huge attraction for visitors. A beautiful octagonal lighthouse, painted white apart from the beacon itself which is housed in red, it seems to encapsulate all that we associate with lighthouses – a friendly sight, a beacon of hope set on a rocky outcrop, defying nature in order to guide ships to safety.

Cape Race, Newfoundland, is one of Canada's most important lighthouses. The original cast-iron tower was built in 1856 on a cliff top 87 feet above the sea. It was maintained by the British government, who charged one-sixteenth of a penny per ton for all ships passing the light. At the beginning of the 20th century the Canadian government took over and cancelled the payable dues. However, as there had been a great increase in shipping traffic, a bigger and better lighthouse was built on the site and, in 1906, the old structure was replaced by a reinforced concrete tower. The 100-foot tower was one of the first reinforced concrete structures in the world and supports one of the biggest lanterns ever made: 28 feet high, 20 feet round and weighing 24 tons, its light can be seen for 24 miles. Cape Race is one of very few lighthouses left in the world that is equipped with a giant hyper-radiant lens that is still in use today. Less than a dozen of these were ever built. It also had a diaphone (compressed air foghorn), at the time a very modern piece of equipment. In 1912 the Cape Race light took the SOS call from the doomed ship *Titanic*.

The original Cape Race light was moved to Cape North, Nova Scotia, in 1908, where it stood for many years before being moved for a third time to Canada's capital, Ottawa, where it now stands guard at a street crossing outside the Museum of Science and Technology. Another example of a lighthouse that has been moved into town is the Queen's Wharf lighthouse that stands at Lakeshore Boulevard and Fleet Street in downtown Toronto. This was originally built on the waterfront in the 1860s, and was moved to its present position in 1929.

In 1867 an act was passed by the British government that established the Dominion of Canada. John A Macdonald was the first prime minister, governing some

3½ million people, most of whom lived in eastern Canada and many of whom were farmers. The amazing achievement of the Canadian Pacific Railway linked the east to the west and, by 1912, all the Canadian provinces had become part of the Dominion except for Newfoundland, which held out until 1949. Many more lighthouses were built in the late 19th century, such as the one at Sable Island, known as 'the graveyard of the Atlantic'. Up until then many keepers houses had stood alone but during this period many keepers' houses were now attached to the towers.

Sable Island lies about 120 miles south of Cape Breton in the midst of the Atlantic. The island itself is just 20 miles long and ¾ mile wide – not much different to the sandbars around it that have brought death and destruction to hundreds of ships over the years. During the 19th century, more than 150 ships were wrecked there and, even now, small vessels do not come within 16 miles of the island because of the danger from submerged sandbars. There are about a dozen people who live on the island, maintaining the two lighthouses that are now sited there to prevent more disasters, as well as a meteorological station. There is also a small herd of wild ponies living on the island that supposedly originate from a ship that went down in the 16th century.

The two lighthouses, placed at the eastern and western ends of the island, were built in 1873. Unfortunately, the western end of the island was being seriously eroded by the sea and, in 1882, it was decided that the lighthouse should be moved to a safer spot. Battling with fierce winds and wild waves, the lantern and housing were safely removed, but sadly a huge wave then hit the side of the tower, which collapsed into the sea. It took until 1888 before its replacement went into service. This time, the 97-foot high octagonal tower, made of reinforced concrete, was placed 2,000 yards from the western end of the island on a small hill about 20 feet above sea level. It and the light at the eastern end of the island still stand today.

Between the 1880s and the 1920s a great deal of lighthouse building took place, due in part to Colonel William Patrick Anderson, the chairman of the Department of Marine and Fisheries Lighthouse Board. Colonel Anderson approved an ambitious building and upgrading programme, not only on the coasts and the St Lawrence River, but also on inland lakes and rivers. Even what is now known as the Northwest Territories had many, largely unmanned, framework towers built, including on the Mackenzie River, the Great Slave Lake and the Hudson Strait.

In 1904, the first maritime wireless station in North America was installed in the prefabricated cast-iron lighthouse at Fame Point on the Gaspé coast. In 1977, this light was moved to Quebec city, where it became a tourist attraction, but it was taken back to its original site in 1997. Also at Cap Gaspé, high above the point at which the St Lawrence River meets the Atlantic Ocean, stands another remote and beautiful lighthouse. Situated in a clearing in the middle of a pristine pine forest, it is close to the edge of a sheer cliff dropping down to the water where, during World War II, the German navy established a secret submarine base.

In the early 20th century, some very exposed reinforced concrete lighthouses were built. They were constructed with buttresses in order to support the higher-order lenses that floated in a mercury bath, and they include Ile Parisienne in Lake Superior and Sheringham Point on Vancouver Island. There are also some very tall reinforced concrete lighthouses, complete with flying buttresses, the finest examples of which are Estevan Point on the Pacific coast and Pointe-au-Père in Quebec. These later buildings mainly retained the octagonal design of the earlier timber lighthouses. Estevan Point is nevertheless extraordinarily modern in appearance, although it was built in 1910. The flying buttresses that support the central tower make it look rather like a rocket about to take off. Colonel Anderson designed the building in this way to protect it from earthquakes as well as wind and waves. One story (possibly apocryphal) attached to Estevan Point, is that in 1942 a Japanese submarine attacked the lighthouse. Apparently some of the shells missed the lighthouse but hit a village of Hesquiat Indians nearby. The Hesquiats immediately organized a war party made up of lots of small speedboats and took off after the submarine, which had to make a hurried escape by putting up a smokescreen and departing under its cover.

In 1913 there was a ferocious storm on Lake Erie during which 12 ships and 235 men were lost. The ornate lighthouse that stands at Point Albino was built in 1917 as a memorial to the crew of US lightship number 82, which sank leaving no survivors.

Electrification of Canadian lighthouses began around 1910, with automation following in the 1940s. By the 1990s, the Canadian Coast Guard had begun to get rid of large numbers of smaller wooden lighthouses because satelitte navigation systems had made them largely redundant. It was at this point that the general public expressed their affection for lighthouses and set about trying to preserve as many as possible. Nowadays, the policy is to help communities take over the care of any light that the Coast Guard deems surplus to requirements, and this has proven a great success. Although there are no longer any manned lighthouses in Nova Scotia, British Columbia has 27.

Point-au-Père, Quebec.

The Romans were responsible for building

the first permanent lighthouses in the British Isles, and indeed there are still a few remains left standing today. According to St Bede, who is known for his *Ecclesiastical History of the English Nation* written in Latin in 731, the Romans built fortified towers to ward off marauding Saxons and Danes, and these doubled up as lighthouses. He tells us that *Streonshalh*, the old name for Whitby, means 'sinus fari' or 'lighthouse bay'. Just a little north of Whitby is a village called Dunsley Bay, in the centre of which is a very old tower that certainly acted as a seamark, if not a lighthouse, for those ancient sailors. The most well-known Roman lighthouse remains, however, are at Dover, where part of an octagonal tower can be seen inside the castle. More remains can be found at Folkestone, Flamborough and St Andrews, and there are also towers at the entrances to Morecambe Bay and Milford Haven.

It is not surprising that Britain has a long association with lighthouses, surrounded as it is by water. Three dangerous reefs lie in wait for the unwary 14 miles off the coast of Plymouth. At high tide, even on the calmest day when the reef is all but submerged, the water rushes and swirls around the central rock, known as the Eddystone. In 1620 the captain of the *Mayflower* wrote about the dangers the reefs presented after successfully managing to avoid them as he shipped the Pilgrim Fathers off to America. As time went on and Plymouth became an increasingly important and busy port, the reefs became more and more problematic – it was not just lives and ships that were being lost there, but precious cargoes, too.

In 1694, King William III and Queen Mary II instructed Trinity House, the guild responsible for lighthouse building from the 16th century on, to build a lighthouse on the

Flamborough, England.

BRITISH ISLES

Eddystone. As a reward, it was allowed to charge a penny each way to all ships going in and out of the harbour. Trinity House came to an agreement with Walter Whitfield of Plymouth, whereby he would finance the building of the lighthouse in exchange for receiving all the lighthouse dues for five years, and half of them for the following 50 years. Luckily for Walter Whitfield, there was a very rich ship owner named Henry Winstanley who was so infuriated by the loss in 1695 of two of his fleet of five ships on the Eddystone that he went to Plymouth to complain to the authorities and demand that a light be put up to rectify the situation.

Henry Winstanley went on to play a greater part in the history of the lighthouse. An artist, designer and inventor, he was well known for his extraordinary practical jokes: chairs that rose into the air or suddenly sank through the floor, carrying the occupant with them, for example. When he was informed that Walter Whitfield was looking for an architect for a lighthouse, he offered his services, despite the fact that one had never before been built on a rock in the middle of the sea.

The lighthouse had to be sited on the one rock on the reef that was still visible at high tide, but one side of the rock was practically vertical and the other side was a very steep slope. Another problem was the fact that it took about six hours each way to get to and from Plymouth, and during the best weather it was still only possible to work on the rock for about three hours each day. Undaunted, he set to work and, by the autumn of 1696, he and his men had managed to put 12 vertical supports into holes bored into the rock itself and fixed there with molten lead.

The following summer, a stone base was built upon which to put the wooden tower. The granite was local and specially cut by stonemasons in Plymouth to fit the slope of the rock. England was at war with France at the time and the Admiralty sent a ship to protect the workers. One day the warship did not appear, and a French ship seized the opportunity to take Winstanley off the rock and over to France as a prisoner. When King Louis XIV was informed, he immediately released Winstanley and sent him back to England, saying: 'I am at war with England, not with humanity.'

The next year was spent building the base, which Winstanley decided to enlarge halfway through the operation. By 1698 it even became possible for the workers to live in the hollow base of the tower, saving themselves the exhausting commute to Plymouth. This significantly speeded the project along, although the weather and working conditions were still atrocious and extremely dangerous. On 14 November 1698 Winstanley lit the tallow candles in the lantern. That winter was the first in living memory when no ships were lost on the Eddystone, but when Winstanley went to look at his work again the following spring, he found that it would have to be greatly strengthened if it was to survive another winter.

The following summer they enlarged the base yet again, and strengthened and heightened the wooden tower. This enabled four more seasons to pass without any loss of shipping, but in the autumn of 1703, Winstanley and his men had to visit the reef to make some urgent repairs. That night the worst storm on record hit the west country: 800 houses and 400 windmills were obliterated, along with over 100 people on land and, allegedly, 8,000 sailors in 150 ships. In the morning, the lighthouse had completely vanished into the sea, taking with it the lighthouse keeper and his family, the workers and Henry Winstanley. Two days later the Eddystone went back to its destructive work, claiming a merchant vessel returning from America and killing all but two of the crew.

In 1705, Trinity House gave permission to Captain John Lovett to build a replacement lighthouse and John Rudyerd was given the task of designing it. He decided that the original lighthouse had not survived because it was too big, strong and solid, and that a slender wooden tower that could give in to the wind would have better luck. This time he made a solid base of wood and stone and a semi-solid tower made of stone with a wooden skin. This contains a staircase that led up to wooden living quarters for the keeper and his family, and was topped by a wooden lantern room. All the wood was caulked in the same way as the hull of a ship.

This second lighthouse lasted for the best part of 50 years, until it suffered the same fate as so many wooden sailing ships: fire. The fire spread extremely quickly and no one could go to the rescue of the three lighthouse keepers because the sea was too rough. They desperately clung to the rock, surrounded by ravaging sea and with flaming debris crashing down around them. One of the keepers, 94-year-old Henry Hall, was looking up at the flaming tower when some molten lead fell into his gaping mouth. Neither of his companions noticed, busy as they were trying to save themselves, and when they were finally rescued, a good eight hours later, none of the rescue party believed Hall's story. He was, however, in bad shape, having first been burned in the fire and then suffering a night of exposure on a freezing cold rock.

When he got to hospital, he told the doctors what had happened, but they did not believe him either – they were convinced he was in shock. Six days later his condition had improved sufficiently for him to sit up in bed and eat a meal, and he continued to improve for another week or so before suddenly dying. Despite his age and the miracle that he had survived at all, his doctor decided to perform a post mortem. To his utter astonishment, there in Hall's stomach was a 7-ounce lump of lead. Far from being an apocryphal story, this piece of lead is on show at Edinburgh's Royal Scottish Museum.

In 1724, the lease of the Eddystone lighthouse was passed to Robert Weston. Realizing how badly a light was needed, he and his partners decided to try to replace it with another structure built to last, regardless of the cost. This time the Royal Society was asked to suggest an engineer who could take on the task, and they quickly suggested John Smeaton.

John Smeaton's plan for the Eddystone lighthouse was that it should be almost monolithic, made of stone and very heavy. Winstanley's original tower appeared to have suffered from the erosion of the pointing of the stonework which had crumbled under the constant lashing of the sea and had never been able to set properly. Smeaton thought that a way around the problem would be to dovetail the stones to ensure rigidity, in the same way that wood could be dovetailed to make a perfect fit. His idea was accepted and he set off to Plymouth to take a closer look at the rock for himself.

During the two months he spent in Plymouth on his first visit, Smeaton only managed to get out to the rock 10 times because of bad weather and high seas. Despite this, he was able to make detailed plans both for the proposed structure itself and for the schedule of works. He also decided to pay high wages in order to attract the best labour force available.

Work began in the late summer of 1756, using every possible hour of decent weather, including the night, plus an 80-ton temporary lightship anchored near the rock to act as quarters for the men, warehouse for materials and, of course, light for shipping. By the end of November, when the workers returned, the rock foundation was ready to

Above: **The Eddystone lighthouse, near Plymouth.**

Opposite: **The Needles, Isle of Wight.**

receive the first blocks of stone. The following summer they laid nine courses of stones, dovetailed, dowelled and tied into each other vertically with 1-foot square marble plugs.

When he returned a year later in 1758, Smeaton was delighted to discover that all nine courses were perfectly in place, and by the end of that season the tower was standing 35 feet above the rock. Work continued and, by August 1759, the 70-foot tower was finished and the words 'Laus Deo' (Praise to the Lord) had been cut into the stone above the door to the lantern room. The ironwork of the lantern and the balcony was then erected and Smeaton himself screwed the gilt ball onto the top of the cupola and finished off the window fittings. The 22 candles in the lantern were finally lit on 16 October 1759 and Smeaton's wonderful, innovative feat of engineering was finished . The tapering circular tower not only stood firm for 140 years but also proved to be the basis for lighthouse building throughout the 19th century. The fame of his lighthouse was such that between 1860 and 1970 it even appeared from time to time on the penny coin.

During the 19th century, however, it became clear that the cement at the bottom of the tower was starting to erode. Robert Stevenson, the great Scottish lighthouse engineer, reported it as being in a dangerous state as early as 1818, but the lighthouse remained untouched for almost 60 years. In 1877, it was decided that Smeaton's lighthouse had to be demolished. It was more than just the cement that had been eroded; the part of the rock upon which the lighthouse stood had also been undermined by the power of the sea. Trinity House's first plan was to blow up the whole reef, so that there would be no need for a lighthouse at all. However, on closer examination they realized that they were talking about the disposal of 2 million tons of rock, and that it would be infinitely more cost effective to build a new lighthouse.

The chief engineer of Trinity House at this time was James Douglass, whose family dominated lighthouse engineering in England throughout the 19th century. He had worked on the lighthouses on Wolf Rock, south west of Land's End, and Bishop's Rock, west of the Scilly Isles, which apart from the Eddystone, are thought to be the most dangerous sites around the English coast. He was now given the task of building the new Eddystone lighthouse. Douglass decided to move the site of the lighthouse to a lower level on the rock, about 120 feet away, and to build it almost twice as high, with a solid cylindrical base rather than a tapering one. The first phase of work involved hacking a level base out of the rock itself, which would be a more difficult task than in previous constructions because of the height of the sea at this lower level. However, Douglass had the advantage over his predecessors of being able to use steamboats. This meant that while fewer hours could be worked per day because of the water level, more weeks could be worked per year because of greater ease of access.

Work began in July 1878 and was able to continue through to December. A level base was made and a watertight structure — a coffer dam — was sunk into the rock itself. This was known as a coffer dam. Once in place, it could be pumped dry so that work could be carried out inside it. As with Smeaton's design, the foundation stones were dovetailed into one another, but this time they were also dovetailed into the reef. To achieve this, the workers had to stand up to their midriffs in water, with ropes tied around them and attached at the other end to boats nearby in case they lost their footing and were swept away. It took the best part of a year to complete the work and pump out the coffer dam, but by the spring of 1880 the granite base they were building stood 2½ feet above the high water level.

At that point, they were able to work on the construction all year round, and by the spring of 1881 they had built a massive 136-foot tower, placed on a solid stone base that was 44 feet in diameter and 22 feet high. The first 23 feet of the tower were also solid stone, and above this there were nine storeys. Over 2,000 blocks of granite were used in building the tower, each one weighing around 2½ tons, and each one being dovetailed into the next on five of its six surfaces. Then, as now, the master of Trinity House was the Duke of Edinburgh, and he duly came to lay the last granite block himself. The Fresnel lamp, lit in May 1882, had the power of 79,250 candles and produced a double flash. Two other lights were situated lower down the tower, beaming directly upon Hands Deep Rock, another danger lying 3½ miles away. In 1959, the light was electrified and now produces the power of 570,000 candles.

James Douglass did his job brilliantly – the project came in almost £20,000 under budget and 18 months before the estimated completion date, and as a result he was awarded a knighthood by Queen Victoria. However, Smeaton's wonderful lighthouse was not by any means forgotten. Considered a national monument of great importance, the upper half, including the lantern room complete with the original candelabra, was taken off and moved to Plymouth Hoe, where it can still be visited. The lower half was filled and topped off neatly and, though dwarfed, is still visible near its more recent companion.

James's father, Nicholas, was also a prominent lighthouse engineer, having built the lighthouse on Bishop's Rock. This was designed by James Walker, who was the chief engineer of Trinity House prior to James Douglass. It was another lethal rock that had claimed many ships, among them three of Sir Cloudesley Shovell's fleet, which were smashed on it in October 1707. Over 2,000 men were drowned in this incident, although Sir Cloudesley himself was washed up alive in Porthellick Cove. Unfortunately for him, Cornish wreckers, aware of the disaster, were waiting on the shore to see what good things the sea would bring them. A woman found the unconscious man and, taking a fancy to a valuable emerald ring he was wearing, murdered him and took the ring for herself. His body was later found and he was buried in Westminster Abbey. The woman eventually confessed to the crime 30 years later and the cleric concerned managed to get the ring back to Sir Cloudesley's family.

The first lighthouse to be placed upon Bishop's Rock consisted of cast-iron legs sunk and braced into the rock itself, which supported an iron platform for the light. This was supposed to allow the ferocious winds and seas to pass through the structure without damaging it. It took three years to erect the lighthouse, and by February 1850 it just needed the light to be positioned when a horrific storm knocked the whole thing down. Nicholas Douglass decided to rethink the entire project, realizing another open structure was pointless. He decided that the new building would have to be a stone tower, no matter how difficult it would be to erect it. He used a similar method to that later used by his son James on the Eddystone – levelling the rock, building a coffer dam and then shaping the granite blocks before taking them out and fixing them on the rock. It took seven years to build this 120-foot tall lighthouse and the light was not lit until 1858.

In 1881, James Douglass reported to Trinity House that his father's tower was being badly damaged by the sea. They decided that not only should the base be strengthened, but that the tower should be heightened as well. In effect, he built a whole new lighthouse around the existing one, and the work was completed in 1887.

As well as designing Bishop's Rock lighthouse, James Walker also designed the tower at Wolf Rock, so called because of the dreadful howling sound that emanated from it. This was actually caused by water rushing into a hollow rock and compressing the air, which made a noise like a wolf's howl when it escaped. James Douglass was the engineer, and he was helped both by his father Nicholas and his brother William. The stonemasons arrived in the spring of 1862 to level the rock and build a landing stage. By 1865 the tower was above the level of the sea, and the light was lit in 1870. There it still stands, seemingly impervious to the power of the ocean. In 1973 it became the first lighthouse to be topped by a helipad, and in 1988 it was made fully automatic.

Sailing to the Isle of Wight from a westerly direction has always been dangerous because of the line of jagged rocks called The Needles and the 400-foot high chalk cliffs that guard the island itself. A great many ships attempting to reach Southampton or Portsmouth have foundered here over the centuries, and as long ago as 1771 Trinity House was petitioned to build a lighthouse. Permission was originally given in 1772 to William Tatnell to erect a lighthouse at his own expense, for an annual recompense of £960 for 21 years. Evidently an agreement suitable to both parties could not be reached because it was Trinity House itself that built the light in 1785. This light was sited on top of the cliffs, and its 10 Argand lamps and reflectors produced a beam that was visible for 11 miles.

It soon became clear, however, that the lighthouse was unsatisfactory. It was often partially hidden by sea mists and fog – something that was true of many lighthouses sited high over the sea, but it was not until 1859, some 70 years and many lost ships later, that Trinity House decided to deal with the situation. James Walker designed the new lighthouse and sited it on the rocks themselves, as far out to sea as possible. The rocks were cut away and levelled to form the foundation, and the cylindrical granite tower that we see today was built for £20,000. To maximize its visibility against the white cliffs behind it, it was painted with red bands and it shows red, green and white lights to help sailors navigate the obstacle course of shoals and banks of which it warns. In 1987 a helipad was put on top of the 102-foot high lighthouse (the keepers had always been brought by boat from Yarmouth), but then in 1994 it was fully automated and controlled from Harwich.

Lowestoft was the first site along England's east coast to be given a lighthouse by Trinity House. In 1609 two towers were built and lit by candles, which paved the way for a string of lights stretching from Norfolk to Kent. The towers were wooden and stood in line, one on the cliff and the other 100 feet below, to mark the deepest water of the Stanford Channel. By 1628 they were in need of repair – so much so that the high light had to be completely rebuilt, and 50 years later the high light was rebuilt yet again, farther back from the headland and on an even higher site. This new light cost £300 to build, and Trinity House, under the management of Samuel Pepys, decided to dispense with the lantern and try an open coal-fired light instead. This proved less than popular with those living nearby, as sparks from the fire were endangering their homes. Trinity House was therefore obliged to place a glazed lantern around the fire, which unfortunately made the light less visible. On completion, Pepys commissioned a plaque showing both the coat of arms of Trinity House and that of his own family. It reads 'Erected by the Brotherhood of the Trinity House of Deptford Strand in the Mastership of Samuel Pepys esq. Secretary of the Admiralty of England Anno Dom 1676'.

The new, higher placement of the Lowestoft lighthouse made it a more important coastal light than it had been, as it could now be seen farther out to sea and did more than show the deep water of the Stanford Channel. Twelve years later it had to be heightened by about 10 feet because houses that had been built near the new tower partially obscured the light. In 1706 the low light was, it is thought, swallowed up by the sea, and it was not replaced until 1730 when an easily movable wooden structure was built. During the 18th century, the low light had to be moved several times as major storms occurred along the coast and the Stanford Channel changed position. Turner painted the Lowestoft lighthouse, and in 1778 when new lighting was put into the high tower, special commemorative mugs were made by the famous Lowestoft pottery, one of which is in London's Victoria and Albert Museum.

During the next hundred years, the Lowestoft lighthouse underwent various changes, including experiments with new lights. A version of today's mirror ball was tried and it lasted for almost 20 years. It was ultimately unsuccessful because, while it glittered, it did not concentrate the beam of light but diffused it instead. Meanwhile, new sandbars grew and vanished and the low light gradually disintegrated and had to be moved. New Argand lights were installed, the low light was rebuilt and new lighthouses were also put up, first in Pakefield and then in Kessingland. The old Pakefield light can still be seen in the grounds of what is now a holiday camp.

In 1867, a new ironwork lighthouse replaced the low light at Lowestoft and, by 1880, both lights were powered by paraffin with revolving lenses that flashed every 30 seconds. By the 1930s, the low light had been dispensed with because the Stanford Channel had disappeared, and the high light was converted to electricity. It had twin optical lenses and became one of the most visible lights on the eastern coast of England.

A light has beamed out to sea from Lowestoft for almost 400 years, and only during the two world wars were there nights when it did not shine, or when every other British lighthouse at the time also went dark. As the oldest lighthouse station in England, Lowestoft is now considered to be one of the most historically precious lighthouse sites in the country.

Farther down the coast lies the charming little town of Southwold. Most of the East Anglian coast is very flat and marshy, but Southwold stands on a more elevated point, so its lighthouse was built at the highest point in the town. In 1887, the brethren of Trinity House agreed that a light should be placed at Southwold because the lower of the two lights at Orford Ness farther south had been swallowed up in a ferocious storm. The coast at Southwold is about 4 miles farther east of Orford Ness and, as it is higher, the light would be more visible.

Construction was to be overseen by James Douglass, and in the meantime a temporary light was placed near the shore at the southern end of the town. The first of more than 1½ million bricks was laid for the permanent lighthouse on 28 May 1889 and, in March 1890, the 8-ton lantern, which had previously been used at Happisburgh in Norfolk, arrived at the port of Harwich. It was brought to Southwold by wagon in two sections and the light was inaugurated on 3 September the same year. It was a new Argand oil burner, of which the lighthouse keepers had no experience. Within a week, there was a fire in the lantern that ruined the new burner. Later that month the light was finally lit successfully.

The Argand burner was replaced first with an incandescent oil lamp and then a paraffin vapour burner, and was finally electrified in 1938. In May 2001, a new optic came

Southwold lighthouse, Suffolk.

into service; its main navigation light is white, and the two red sectors mark shoals lying to the north and south. The tower itself is a listed building, and stands a splendid 101 feet high, its gleaming white paint a perfect foil for the many pretty pastel-coloured cottages around it.

On the opposite side of the country from East Anglia lies Wales, and the oldest lighthouse on the Welsh coast stands at St Anne's Head at the entrance to Milford Haven. In 1662 Trinity House agreed that a coal-fired light should be placed there, and the private owners were told that it should be supported by voluntary payments. Within six years, parliament ordered the light to be extinguished when it discovered that the owners were illegally demanding payments from ship owners. However, the light was essential because it guided shipping into the harbour and also warned of Linney Head and its two dangerous rocks, Crow Rock and Toes Rock. While no other light existed on the west coast of England or Wales at this time, nothing was done to remedy the situation for 45 years.

In 1713 Trinity House was petitioned for a new light at St Anne's Head and granted Joseph Allen a 99-year lease on the erection of two lights for an annual rent of £10. He was allowed to levy one penny per ton of cargo from British ships entering the harbour, and two pence from foreign ships. Two lights were built in order to show the way past the two rocks and to prevent ships from confusing the lights with the single light at St Agnes in the Isles of Scilly. Construction began before the lease was signed – showing how desperately the lights were needed – and they were lit by the summer of 1714.

In 1800 Trinity House bore the cost of installing new Argand lights, which was repaid from the lighthouse dues, and in 1801 Robert Stevenson wrote a glowing report on the state of the lighthouses during his first lighthouse tour. The lease reverted to Trinity House in 1813, but the lower front light had to be rebuilt in 1844 due to erosion of the cliff. The new lighthouse was placed 30 feet back from the cliff edge and stands there to this day, 43 feet high with an octagonal tower. The high light some way behind it was closed down and converted to a coastguard station in 1910. During the 1980s and 1990s, four lighthouse keepers manned St Anne's Head, and after the automation of The Smalls, Skokholm and South Bishop, they also supported helicopter operations to those remote lights as well. In 1998 St Anne's Head itself was automated, and like so many others is now controlled from Harwich. Trinity House, however, still uses it as an operating base for its maintenance teams.

The Smalls is a reef situated 21 miles off St David's Head and is the most westerly point of Wales. The first lighthouse on The Smalls was built and lit in 1776 by a Quaker from Liverpool named John Phillips 'for the great and holy good to serve and save humanity'. However, the winter of 1777 was particularly bad, and as he could not afford to repair the lighthouse, he handed it over to some Liverpool traders, who in turn passed it to Trinity House. They granted Phillips a 99-year lease on his lighthouse at £5 annual rental. In 1800 one of the two keepers died of natural causes. His colleague was so scared of being accused of murder that he ripped up some of the interior panels of the lighthouse and built a coffin. Placing the corpse inside it, he lashed the coffin to the exterior of the lantern where it stayed for three weeks until the relief ship arrived. Subsequently, it was decided that there should be a minimum of three keepers on every isolated rock station. In the event, Trinity House bought out the lease to The Smalls in 1836, and John Phillips' family received just over £170,000 in compensation. It had been

St Anne's Head lighthouse, Wales.

a very good investment. In 1859 James Douglass designed a new granite tower because the original tower was in such a bad state. The new tower was completed in 1861 and was the first to boast an internal lavatory. This is the tower we can see today.

Skokholm is an island lying about 5 miles off St Anne's Head. A small island, its lighthouse was not built until 1916, but stands in a spectacular position by the edge of high red sandstone cliffs. A bird sanctuary, the island receives many visits from scientists and students. The lighthouse there was automated in 1983, and in 1998 was converted to solar power. Before conversion, the light had been changed from red to white and, to the dismay of the Royal Society for the Protection of Birds (RSPB), a great many birds, attracted to the white light, flew straight into the glass lantern and died. When solarization was introduced, red shades were used to cover the island section of the light, and this appears to have largely solved the problem.

South Bishop is a remote rock lying about 5 miles south west of St David's Head. It is the largest of a scattered group of rocks known as the Bishops and Clerks. The first petition that Trinity House received for the building of a lighthouse here was in 1831, followed by another petition three years later, prompting them to start work. Built by James Walker, the lighthouse was completed by 1839 and still uses the original lantern – the oldest working lantern in England and Wales. Diesel generators were added in 1959, allowing electrification, and a helipad was built on a lower, flat piece of the rock in 1971. Fully automated in 1983, the lighthouse is now controlled from Harwich. In 2000 solar panels were added to the site, which are now the sole source of power. South Bishop lighthouse, like Skokholm, has also suffered the problem of birds flying into the lantern, as it stands directly on the migration route of various species. In a joint effort, Trinity

House and the RSPB placed numerous perches around the lantern, which has helped but not entirely solved the problem.

On the north-east point of Anglesey stands the unusual looking Point Lynas lighthouse. In the latter half of the 18th century, as trade with America began to boom and Liverpool became an important port, a boarding station was established at Point Lynas for the pilots who guided shipping into the Mersey River. At first, the pilots kept a look-out from a farmhouse on the point, but in 1779 William Hutchinson, who was the harbour master at Liverpool, set up his own lighthouse on the point. Unfortunately, it was not sufficiently visible and, after a ship named the *Rothesay Castle* foundered there, the Mersey Docks and Harbour Company employed Jesse Hartley to build a better structure. By 1835, he had built the low-lying castellated lighthouse that we see today. Painted white, the lantern room is at ground level and attached to the main body of the building. Trinity House took over the lighthouse in 1973, and now it is fully automated, using mains electricity but with back-up generators in case of power failure. It shows a white light and has a fog detector device that automatically sounds the fog signal whenever necessary.

Farther north, just south of the harbours of Whitehaven, Workington and Maryport, is St Bees lighthouse. Situated on a high headland, this small, pretty little lighthouse was built to help guide ships between north Wales, Liverpool, the Isle of Man and the Solway Firth. In 1718, Trinity House received a petition to erect a lighthouse there, and leased it for 99 years to Thomas Lutwige for £20 per annum. Thomas Lutwige built the lighthouse himself, and it is thought to have been made of the local sandstone. Lutwige was able to levy dues of three-and-a-half pence per ton of cargo from all ships entering the local ports. He built a 30-foot high round tower that was 16 feet in diameter,

South Bishop lighthouse, Wales.

on top of which he placed an open metal grate. The keepers had to keep the fire topped up with coal, and to avoid inhaling too much smoke there were ladders situated at intervals all the way around. This enabled them to climb up whichever ladder was in a smoke-free zone, but as it was such hard work, especially when it was windy, they were paid the handsome sum of seven shillings a week.

Robert Stevenson wrote of his visit to St Bees that the grate was quite small – only 2 feet deep and 2 feet in diameter at the top – and that it used about 130 tons of coal per year. It was not very satisfactory and Lutwige was frequently harassed by ship owners who complained that on windy nights the light was often obscured by smoke. In 1822, the tower burned down and Trinity House decided to rebuild it in stone. That same year the new 56-foot high, white-painted tower was completed, and its new oil lights were lit. St Bees was the last British lighthouse to use a coal fire. It was automated in 1987 and the keepers' cottages that stand between the tower and the edge of the cliff were sold off by Trinity House the following year.

In 1810, Trinity House held a meeting with the Blackett family, who owned the lease on the Farne Islands off the coast of Northumberland, and arranged for two new lighthouses to be built by Daniel Alexander – one on Inner Farne and one on Outer Farne, otherwise known as Longstone. Alexander's lighthouse on Longstone was built to contain one of the first lights in the world that both flashed and revolved. By 1822 Trinity House, enabled by an act of parliament, had bought the site and employed Joseph Nelson to enlarge and improve upon the existing lighthouse. This he did, and in 1827 a fine stone tower – 85 feet high, painted red with a central band of white and boasting a light comprising 12 Argand lamps, parabolic reflectors and a cadioptric lens – was lighting the way for ships sailing around the north-east coast of England. The improvements cost over £6,000 and William Darling, together with his wife, son and daughter, moved onto the bleak, rocky little island to tend the light. William came from a lighthouse-keeping family. His father, Robert, had been the keeper on Brownsman Island, another of the Farne Islands, in 1795. On his death, William took over to become the first keeper of the Longstone light. The Darling family came to national prominence in 1838, thanks to William's daughter, Grace. William's wife was ill, and his son worked on the mainland, so he was assisted by his 22-year-old daughter. William and Grace Darling were alone at the lighthouse on the night of 6 September when a bad storm blew up. *The Forfarshire*, a passenger steamer carrying 63 people from Hull to Dundee, was caught up in the high winds, which drove the ship onto Big Harkar rock, ½ mile from the lighthouse. The ship broke up spectacularly, and 50 people were drowned within minutes. The remaining 13 managed to cling onto the rock they had foundered upon and spent the rest of the night fighting for their lives, soaked by the pounding waves, freezing cold and in despair. Four of them perished during the night.

When daylight broke, Grace Darling looked out of her window and saw the wreckage and the pathetic group of survivors huddled on the rock. Having woken her father, they both decided to make a rescue attempt, using their small little flat-bottomed fishing boat. Rowing out through the stormy waters, they finally reached the rock; Grace had to keep the boat alongside without wrecking it as well, while her father went onto the rock to help people from it to the boat. The boat was only small and could not hold all nine people, so Grace and her father not only had to struggle back to the lighthouse with the first group, but then had to turn around and go back for the remainder. They successfully rescued all nine people, and then had to look after them in the lighthouse for two more days until the storm abated.

Grace Darling became nationally famous. She was the subject of at least one song of the day, and hundreds of people from all over England made trips to the Farne Islands to see her and the setting of this heroic deed. Unfortunately, Grace, who had lived a very sheltered life until this point, contracted tuberculosis and died four years later in 1842. Longstone lighthouse, however, survives and was fully automated in 1990; it is controlled from the Trinity House control centre in Harwich.

Twin lighthouses at Whitby harbour, Yorkshire.

Longstone lighthouse, Northumberland.

Scotland has a magnificent, wild coastline that

stretches for some 6,000 miles. It boasts hundreds of islands, fearsome rocks and mountains that sweep down to the sea, creating fantastic visual scenery that can rival any other coastline in the world. It also poses extreme difficulties for mariners – to the extent that there were no sea charts of Scotland prior to 1583. It also suffers from frequent bad weather conditions and this is perhaps why the first lighthouse, on the Isle of May in the middle of the Firth of Forth, was not built until 1636. There were, of course, early lights lit on headlands and shores, but those fires would not have been visible to anyone other than local fishermen. The first lighthouse stood for 180 years until the Northern Lighthouse Board commissioned a replacement which was finished in 1816. Originally a coal-fired light, it was fully automated in 1989.

In 1786, parliament passed an act 'for erecting certain lighthouses in the Northern Parts of Great Britain'. The act required the building of four lighthouses at Kinnaird Head, North Ronaldsay, the Mull of Kintyre and Eilean Glas, and fixed the dues that could be collected to one penny per ton of cargo from British ships and two pennies per ton from foreign ships. Only whaling ships and those making the journey around the Scandinavian coast to Archangel in Russia were exempt from the charge. The act also created an independent board of commissioners and trustees to organize lighthouse building and management in Scotland – the Northern Lighthouse Board.

The board appointed a lamp maker named Thomas Smith as its chief engineer. He had already produced a light using an Argand glass chimney and a parabolic reflector, and he promptly travelled to England to learn about the construction of lighthouses. His stepson was Robert Stevenson, and Smith quickly hired

Isle of May, Scotland.

Robert as his assistant and apprentice engineer. At only 15 years of age, Robert accompanied Smith in his work on the Kinnaird Head and Mull of Kintyre lighthouses. Robert later married one of Smith's daughters and together they began an extraordinary lighthouse-building dynasty.

Robert Stevenson went on to become one of the greatest lighthouse engineers in history. By the time he was 26, he was fully qualified and in 1799 he took over from his stepfather as chief engineer to the Northern Lighthouse Board. By that time, he had been involved in the building of several lighthouses, although only one of his own. His ambition was to build a lighthouse on Bell Rock, a calamitous red sandstone reef lying well out to sea between the Firth of Tay and the Firth of Forth.

According to legend, Bell Rock was named when a certain John Gedy, the abbott of Aberbrothock in the 14th century, hung a bell on the rock. The bell rang constantly because of the wind and the waves and warned sailors of the hidden danger lying in wait for them. The reef certainly took a great many ships and their crews down to their deaths, but it was considered impossible to build upon it – not only does it lie some 11 miles out to sea, but it is also submerged to a depth of 16 feet twice a day. Farmers living near the mainland coast were said to fence their yards in fine hardwoods and to wash down their porridge with the finest cognacs – their farms were far more valuable than those inland because of the exceedingly rich harvests they could reap from the sea.

For eight long years, Robert Stevenson pushed the board to allow him to build the lighthouse, and finally in 1807 work began. Teams of men were hired at very high wages. They had to live on board a ship that was anchored near the rock until a barracks was built on the rock itself. Their daily ration of food was generous – ½ pound of beef per day, along with oatmeal, bread, butter, vegetables, barley and 6 pints of beer. They also received a ration of rum whenever the weather was wet or cold, or when they had been forced to work longer hours than usual. The first thing to do was to build a forge and secure it to the rock – of course, the blacksmith had to work up to his knees in water, and the sea could easily rush in and put out his fire. Nevertheless, by 10 July 1808 the foundation was complete.

The tower Stevenson designed was based on the Eddystone, but would stand at least 30 feet higher. By August 1810, 2,835 granite rocks had been used to complete the newly built lighthouse at a cost of over £60,000 – hugely over budget. However, when the rotating oil lamp was lit, its red and white beams could be seen from 25 miles away and both the Northern Lighthouse Board and the general public thought it was worth every penny.

Robert Stevenson had three sons, Alan, Thomas and David, all of whom built lighthouses, as did his grandsons. The only exception was his grandson, Robert Louis Stevenson, who went into engineering and completed his studies before turning his back on the lighthouse-building business. However, Robert Louis Stevenson was proud of his heritage. In 1880 he wrote: 'Whenever I smell salt water I know that I am not far from one of the works of my ancestors. The Bell Rock stands monument for my grandfather, the Skerry Vore for my Uncle Alan and when the lights come out at sundown along the shores of Scotland, I am proud to think they burn brightly for the genius of my father.' Among the various lighthouses built by Robert Stevenson, Barra Head deserves particular attention. Built in 1833, it is situated off the coast of Barra in the Outer Hebrides. This is a truly remote and beautiful lighthouse, the highest in the British Isles and exceedingly difficult to reach. The actual building was not difficult to construct, as the tower is only 59 feet high, but getting the building materials to the site must have been an extraordinary effort. Everything was brought by ship and then hauled by hand up 625 feet of sheer cliff face. One has to hope that the three keepers and their families got on well together, as they were virtually marooned on this isolated rock with no one else to talk to and nowhere else to go. Barra Head was automated in 1980.

Between them, the Stevenson family built 97 magnificent lighthouses. Alan Stevenson's greatest feat was probably the lighthouse at Skerryvore. His father, Robert, had dreamed of building a lighthouse on the rocks at Skerryvore to aid the ships sailing to and from Ireland and America using the ports of Oban, Glasgow and Liverpool, as well as more local traffic, which was coming to grief there on a regular basis. In the 54 years before the light was finally lit, 30 ships foundered on the 8 miles of reef, south of Tiree.

In 1814, Robert Stevenson and the writer Walter Scott managed to land on the reef, and Scott noted: 'The rock was carefully measured by Mr S. It will be a most desolate position for a lighthouse – the Bell Rock and Eddystone a joke to it, for the nearest land is the wild island of Tiree, at 14 miles' distance.' Although Stevenson's report stated that it would be possible to build on the reef, the scheme never got off the ground because it was thought to be too dangerous and difficult.

In 1834, Alan Stevenson visited Skerryvore for a second look and, having mapped the reef, he proposed the highest and heaviest lighthouse that had ever been built. This proposal was accepted, and Robert Stevenson, who was well into his 60s by then, put

Alan in charge of the project. Until this point, Alan's major contribution to lighthouse construction was his work on lights, particularly his important refinements to the Fresnel lens. Alan began work in 1837 by building a jetty built on the Isle of Mull – about 20 miles from Tiree. Mull had quantities of good-quality granite. A harbour was built at Tiree to enable the stone and other materials to be transported there, and a structure on iron stilts was built on the rocks themselves to house the workers. All this took a year of arduous work, but overnight in November 1838 the ocean took the workers' house – luckily empty at the time. The following year was spent rebuilding the living quarters and blasting out a 42-foot diameter foundation pit for the tower.

The granite stones were landed at Tiree and shaped in situ. The easiest took 85 hours to shape and the most difficult up to 320 hours. Almost 4,500 stones had to be shaped and taken to the reef. The working conditions on the rock itself were horrendous, and the living just as bad – 30 men at any one time cramped together in a house built on 40-foot high stilts that swayed in the wind and was breached by the foam from the waves. Alan lived and worked right there with them. Given the conditions it is amazing that no serious accidents occurred during the six years they worked there.

By the end of 1840, the tower had risen to a height of only 8 feet, but one year later it was almost 60 feet high. In 1843 Alan, whose health was failing, was made chief engineer of the Northern Lighthouse Board, taking over from his father, and he gave the job of finishing Skerryvore to his brother, Thomas. Alan's health never recovered from the privations he had suffered when working on the Skerryvore light and he soon resigned from his job. It was filled by his younger brother, David, and Thomas soon shared it with him.

Skerryvore was inaugurated on 1 February 1844, and had cost as much to build as a warship. Considered to be an almost perfect structure, this elegantly tapered rock tower stands 138 feet high. The walls are 9½ feet thick at the bottom and 2 feet thick at the top. It contains nine rooms, one on top of the other, each 12 feet in diameter and accessed by ladders. Stevenson used the weight of the solid base and the 4,500 stones to anchor Skerryvore firmly to the rocks. In 1954, a fire destroyed the lighting apparatus, but the tower survived and the light was replaced. Skerryvore was fully automated in 1994, and the four lighthouse keepers' cottages on Tiree were acquired by the Hebridean Trust for use as affordable homes for island families.

The lighthouse at the Mull of Kintyre was another of the four lighthouses that the Northern Lighthouse Board was required to build by the act of 1786, and it is the second of the four to have been erected. It was designed by Thomas Smith, the board's first chief engineer, and, although it is built on the tip of the headland 240 feet above the sea, it is sited in such a remote spot that even today it is difficult to reach. All the raw materials for the building work and the builders themselves were brought from Campbeltown, 12 miles away, and landed at Carskiey, a small inlet about 5 miles away. To reach it, there was a full day's journey across the peninsula using pack animals. Rebuilt in the early 19th century, it became world famous when Paul McCartney wrote a song about it – he had fallen in love with the lighthouse and its beautiful surroundings. The flashing light, now powered by solar panels, can still be seen from over 25 miles away.

The most northerly lighthouse in the British Isles is Muckle Flugga. Standing on a barren rock 200 feet above the Atlantic Ocean and just north of the Isle of Unst in the

Muckle Flugga is the home of the most northerly light in the UK.

Shetlands, it is farther north than St Petersburg and the Alaskan Peninsula. It is one of the few lighthouses that came into being as a result of war rather than peace. In 1854, Britain was at war with Russia in the Crimea and, to prevent Russian ships from sailing around the north of Scotland, the coastline had to be patrolled. Britain also wanted to blockade the Russian fleet's own northern ports, but the whole enterprise was exceedingly dangerous because the coastline is littered with reefs, rocks and islands.

The politics of building the lighthouse at North Unst meant that agreement had to be reached between the Northern Lighthouse Board, Trinity House and the Board of Trade. Despite this difficulty, in March 1854 David Stevenson was dispatched to select a spot upon which to build. He hit such terrible seas that he reurned saying it was impossible to build there at all. Refusing to give up, Trinity House then sent a committee to see for themselves a couple of months later. They were lucky enough to have decent weather and a fairly calm sea and, of course, thought that building there would be perfectly possible. After yet another visit by the Northern Lighthouse Board, a compromise was reached, and the decision was taken to erect a temporary light.

The work began in September, and the engineers started to hew out a flat area on top of the rock upon which to place the light. This was done by hand; the men then cut steps into the side of the rock to give them easier access and to enable materials to be dragged up to the top. A combination of the urgency of the war and the encroaching winter galvanized everyone so much that a temporary lighthouse was up and running within four weeks.

Two years later, as a result of wave damage to the structure, it was decided to erect a permanent building on the site. Having persuaded the workers that it would be more efficient if they could work all winter, the first thing to be constructed was a large iron house for the workers and their tools and rations. The workers felt quite secure in their house, 200 feet above the sea, but in December, just as they were settling down to their breakfast, a huge wave came up the rock, burst open their door, soaking them to the skin and sweeping away what it could back through the door and out to sea. Moments later the horrified workers suffered another huge wave that this time almost knocked off their iron roof.

When they reported this story to the engineers, Thomas and David Stevenson, it was decided that an enormous stone wall should be built around the lighthouse to break the force of any large waves that might damage it. The Stevensons also decided that the lighthouse would have to be made of brick because of the difficulty of transporting materials to the top of this uncompromising rock – this would be the first time a lighthouse in such an exposed site would be built of brick. The 64-foot tower, painted white, was finished and lit on 1 January 1858. The lighthouse was automated in 1995 and is today tended by helicopter.

The first real authority for lighthouses in Ireland was

the Commissioners of Barracks in Dublin, formed in 1767 and largely made up of officers in the army or navy. They were responsible only for the building of lighthouses – the lights themselves were the responsibility of the customs authority. Taking advantage of their new powers, the customs officers soon began to embezzle the funds intended for lighthouses. However, they were so blatant in this abuse that they were caught and punished and their responsibilities were passed to the Ballast Board in Dublin. The Ballast Board was very slow about taking any action at all, but by 1800 eight lighthouses were in place around the Irish coast. In 1867, the board became the Commissioners of Irish Lights.

As long ago as the 5th century, the Celtic monks of St Dubham supposedly lit fires at the south east of Ireland, close to where Hook Head lighthouse stands today at the entrance to Waterford Harbour in County Wexford. Certainly a fortified tower, dungeon and lighthouse were built on the same site circa 1172, probably by invading Normans. This makes it far and away the oldest lighthouse in Ireland – indeed, it is the oldest working light in the British Isles. It is recorded that by 1245, the Augustinians had charge of the tower and were permitted to collect dues from ships coming in and out of the harbour in exchange for maintaining the tower and the light.

By the 17th century the light was no longer working but by 1665, after many petitions from local sailors, Sir Robert Reading was given the authority to get it up and running again. With walls that were 80 feet tall and 10 feet thick, the stone tower itself, standing 59 feet high, was still in pretty good shape, but the shortish upper section and the lantern itself were added by Sir Robert in the 1670s. He was able to collect lighthouse

Hook Head lighthouse, county Wexford, Ireland.

dues, but in 1704, after it was discovered that he had been overcharging, he was obliged to return the lighthouse to the Crown, after which an additional £87 or so were spent on repairs. In 1791, a larger lantern and better lights were installed. During the 19th century, some serious renovations were required and a central turret was added. Standing 151 feet above sea level, this imposing black and white banded tower was automated in 1996, and a visitors centre was opened there in 2001.

Farther around the south coast of Ireland lies a small island, just off the coast of County Waterford, home of Ballycotton lighthouse. Built in 1851 by George Halpin, it stands 194 feet above sea level, although the actual tower is only 49 feet tall. George Halpin and his son George Jr between them built over 50 lighthouses and are two of Ireland's most famous lighthouse engineers.

In 1845, George Sr was recorded as an inspector, but on his death in 1864 he was called engineer. His son built fewer towers than his father, but they must have worked together on many. George Jr was recorded as his father's assistant in 1830 and took over from him in 1849. He died just a few years after his father in 1860. George Sr was responsible for Tuskar and Great Skellig lighthouses among others, and George Jr's most famous lighthouse is Fastnet. Ballycotton could well have been built by the pair of them, and it certainly looks extraordinary − painted black to show up against the blue sky and the green grass, it is enclosed by a big stone wall. Its light flashes red and white, and when red makes the place look mysterious and somewhat sinister.

The Fastnet light is Ireland's most famous lighthouse. Situated out to sea about 5 miles off the south-west tip of the country, it rises almost organically from its rocky base. For thousands of Irish emigrants to the United States, it was the last piece of Ireland

Ballycotton island, Ireland.

that they saw, which earned it the name 'the teardrop of Ireland'. In Celtic, 'fastnet' meant 'farewell' and many people consider it to be one of the most beautiful lighthouses in the world.

In 1848, George Halpin Jr began to build the first Fastnet lighthouse, which was sited right at the top of the crag. A six-year project resulted in a cast-iron structure about 20 feet in diameter and 64 feet high. The keepers had separate quarters on the north-east side of the rock, but even though they built at the highest point possible, the keepers soon began to complain that the tower moved and shook during stormy weather and they feared that it might collapse. On one particularly rough day, the sea tore a huge piece of rock weighing several tons from the cliff and then tossed it straight at the tower with the next surge.

By the early 1860s, it was decided that the tower had to be strengthened because it was becoming unsound. A casing was built around the base of the tower to two storeys high, and rocks dumped between it and the original tower for additional strength. The two storeys of the tower were filled in and the upper storeys made into the keepers' new dwellings. Their original house was abandoned. This new reinforced tower was much stronger and stood up to the force of the waves without flinching for about 30 years. Then an incident occurred that made the Commissioners of Irish Lights think yet again – an enormously high sea reached right up and smashed the exterior glass of the lantern itself, damaging one of the lenses.

William Douglass was the chief engineer to the Commissioners of Irish Lights at this time, having previously worked for Trinity House for 26 years. He recommended and designed a completely new tower, made of Cornish granite and built upon a ledge of rock

The Fastnet lighthouse, Ireland.

that was 6 inches below high water level. Work began in the late 1890s. This was an even more difficult construction job than the original tower, as both workers and materials had to be landed on the ledge and attached by lines strung between the ledge and the supply ship. The ship could not be moored too close by because the swell would keep smashing it against the rock itself. The granite pieces, each between 4 and 5 tons in weight, were cut and dovetailed on shore, packed into wooden crates and brought out on the ship. A derrick was rigged up on the rock itself, with a long boom with a rope on the end of it that swung out to the boat. The rope was attached to a crate and then the crate was carefully lowered into the sea, brought to the foot of the tower and lifted onto the ledge. Over 2,000 pieces of granite were landed in this fashion during the course of four years.

The foreman, James Kavanagh, barely left the site throughout the work. Twice he stayed on the rock for a year at a time and the workers had shore leave just once every three months. The tapered tower was 177 feet high with a 52-foot diameter base. The tower itself was completed in 1903, and work began on installing the lantern immediately afterwards.

Having successfully landed the lantern and apparatus, and heaved it up the rock to a safe place, an enormous storm arrived and swamped everything, including the lantern and all its parts, most of which vanished into the sea overnight. As there was no possibility of getting a new lantern for several months, the old lantern was transferred to the new tower and shone out for another year. Finally, in 1904, the new lantern was put in place. It was a new type of oil light – the oil was pressurized and produced gas, which was fed to Bunsen burners. The light this produced was then intensified by dioptric lenses, giving a very powerful beam. Kavanagh never saw the new light, however – worn out by his years on the rock, he went ashore feeling ill and died of a stroke shortly before it was lit for the first time.

In 1912 this magnificent, elegant lighthouse was the last piece of land that the passengers of the ill-fated *Titanic* saw as they left for the United States. Many of their bodies were washed up near the Sambro Island lighthouse and buried in Halifax, Nova Scotia. The grave of Jack, the young man played by Leonardo diCaprio in the film *Titanic*, is almost a place of pilgrimage today, visited by thousands of young people and decorated with flowers and photographs of Kate Winslet. Fastnet lighthouse was automated in 1989 and now has a helipad, an automatic foghorn and a white flashing light that is visible for up to 27 miles.

Another remarkable lighthouse built on a remote rock in the sea is Skellig Michael, off the south-west coast of Ireland in County Kerry. In fact, there are two rocks and two lighthouses, the larger one housing the light. In the 6th century a monastery was built there, the remains of which can still be seen today. The first lighthouse to be built there, completed in 1826, was designed by George Halpin Sr. It comprised a fine stone tower with separate keepers' cottages, surrounded by a hefty stone wall. Built on a ledge halfway up a towering cliff face, this building lasted for the best part of 140 years, but the lighthouse that we see today was built in a different position in 1967 and was reached by a path that snakes around the cliffs. Automated in 1987, it has a visibility range of 27 miles, and nowadays it also has a helipad that makes life considerably easier for visiting technicians.

Fanad Head, another of George Halpin Sr's designs, was constructed in 1817. Situated at the entrance to Lough Swilly on the north coast of Ireland, it started out as a

Fanad Head, Ireland

lighthouse of not very great significance. It has become a substantial site, however, with sizable and comfortable accommodation, and is indeed still lived in. It is the helicopter base for all the offshore lighthouses in Northern Ireland, and although it was automated in 1978, there is so much activity there that it is still manned by a keeper and his family. The keeper actually lives in the nearby town but checks on all the equipment and accommodates visiting technicians and helicopter crew members on their way to and from other jobs. The lighthouse itself is 72 feet high and 128 feet above sea level. Its white flashing light is visible for 18 miles and its red flash for 14 miles.

The elegance and beauty of French lighthouse design
is acknowledged throughout the world. Unlike the sometimes severe and functional grandeur
of many of the famous British and North American towers, the French dedication to art,
fashion and beauty has influenced lighthouse construction as much as everything else.
Around the French coast are towers reflecting architectural styles as diverse as Baroque –
Cordouan, for example – and Art Deco – Petite Foule in the Vendee, for instance. The vast
majority of the beautiful structures contain nothing more than a staircase leading up to the
control room, with the keepers living in more modest, separate dwellings.

Cordouan light has a noble history. Set at the mouth of the Gironde estuary, which is
buffeted by prevailing winds from the Atlantic, many of the sailing ships engaged in
transporting wine from Bordeaux were wrecked on the constantly shifting sandbanks. During
the 9th century, the citizens of Bordeaux were sufficiently concerned to send a petition to
Emperor Charlemagne's son, Louis the Pious, for permission to erect a light at the entrance
to the river. This light remained there until 1409, when Edward, the Black Prince, had a stone
tower built in its place.

Almost 200 years passed and the tower had fallen into ruin when King Henry III
charged the architect Louis de Foix with building a new lighthouse. Louis de Foix designed a
lighthouse fit for a king, complete with royal apartments and a chapel, and work began in 1584.
The building was hugely ambitious, and as the sea was eroding the spit of land upon which the
lighthouse stood, de Foix spent the first few years building defences against it. The king died
five years into the project and was succeeded by Henry IV, then Louis XIII. In 1602, Louis de
Foix also died and his son, Pierre, worked on it until 1606, when his father's foreman, François

La Coubre
light, France.   FRANCE, PORTUGAL AND SPAIN

Beuscher, took over and finished the job in 1611, 27 years after the start of the project and nine years before the Pilgrim Fathers set sail for America.

The Cordouan lighthouse was a masterpiece. Sometimes referred to as the Versailles of the sea, its decorative splendour was purely a visual extravaganza serving no practical need. Its richly decorated interior included Etruscan pilasters encircling the lowest stage and a staircase of some 91 feet in diameter winding upwards to the King's Hall, with a vaulted ceiling and marble floor. Up again, the staircase climbed to the unique, ornately decorated King's Chapel, into which light poured from seven dormer windows in the dome, sadly no longer there. The third floor was topped by an openwork balustrade, and at the top was the stone lantern in which a wood fire burned at night.

By 1664, sperm whale oil was used for the lamp, but by 1717 it had severely damaged the lantern. Ten years later, a new cast-iron lantern was installed, burning coal from England. By the 1780s, the building was falling into disrepair and the land on which it stood was being ravaged by the sea. The businessmen of Bordeaux demanded a higher tower, and renovations were begun in 1785 and completed in 1789, just as the French Revolution started. Joseph Teulere took down everything above the chapel and built a circular stone tower with a lantern and an Argand lamp, making the lighthouse a tremendous 197 feet high.

In 1813 the French government finally appointed a lighthouse authority, as it had become clear that they were falling behind both Britain and North America as regards lighthouse building. Augustin Jean Fresnel was able to use the Cordouan light as a place in which to experiment with his lenses, and in 1823 it became the first lighthouse in the world to be set up with the new Fresnel system. Once again, the lighthouse was allowed to deteriorate and, in 1853, the French government, which had recently declared the

Il Vierge lighthouse, France.

lighthouse to be a historic monument, ordered the chapel to be rebuilt perfectly on the first floor, stained glass windows and all, and a new, improved optic to be installed. In 1948 the light was electrified and, since then, there has been a steady trickle of modernization. Its white flashing light is visible for 27 miles and it also has a red and green secondary light.

Les Roches Douvres lies between the Channel Islands and north-east Finistère. It is the first structure that French ships come across after setting sail south east from England. Standing on a reef about 20 miles from land, it is the most isolated lighthouse in Europe. In 1867, a metal tower was erected that lasted until World War II, when it was destroyed by the Germans. The lighthouse keepers must have been relieved to see it go, as for almost 80 years they had lived and worked in dreadful conditions. The tower was made of sheets of metal bolted onto a metal frame. It was always wet with condensation running down the walls, and when the weather was bad, the tower swayed in the wind and made a horrendous noise.

The enormous, grandiose stone lighthouse we see today is quite recent – built between 1948 and 1954, it stands 197 feet high and has the air of a much older structure, possibly due to its design and the fact that it is made of the natural pink granite that is found in Finistère. Fully automated, its beacon can be seen from 28 miles away. It has a helipad and two modern windmills close by on the rocks, which were pioneered by the French lighthouse authority, the Bureau des Phares et Balises.

The Ile Vierge lighthouse was built in 1902 on the island of the same name, near Finistère, and, at 269 feet high, is the tallest lighthouse in Europe. Standing guard over a series of dangerous reefs, rocks and islets, it needs to be visible from a long distance. The original square tower and dwelling were built in 1845 and still stand close to today's tower. Equipped with a helipad, its powerful Fresnel optic beams out over the sea to help keep seafarers safe and sound. Keeper Jean Malgorne is one of only four lighthouse keepers left in France. He has lived and worked for 28 years in the tower dubbed 'Purgatory', despite its beautiful wood panelling and the 12,500 sheets of opaline that tile the walls of the vast stairwell. Its nickname is due to its bleak physical situation, as well as the 397 steps that have to be climbed to reach the control room.

La Vielle, meaning 'old lady', is another outstanding lighthouse. Set upon a rocky outcrop 1 mile from the coast at south Finistère, it has stood as one of a series of lighthouses and navigational lights that guard the Atlantic coast of France. Built in 1887 and standing 88 feet high, it is a marvellous castellated tower that looks like a chessboard castle. Automated in 1995, it has red, white and green flashing lights. Despite its proximity to the shore, it has had to survive a great deal of appallingly bad weather and even worse seas. Two keepers, Mandolini and Terraci, were once imprisoned in La Vielle for three months before efforts to relieve them were successful.

La Coubre light, in the Charente Maritime, stands on the northern point of the entry to the Gironde, the river that runs down to Bordeaux. Originally built in 1860, and largely rebuilt 35 years later, the tower we see today was erected in 1905. The surrounding area is extremely flat and the tower was sited about a mile inland in an effort to avoid the erosion that has brought the waves to within a mere 800 feet or so over the last 100 years. An elegantly tapered tower painted white for the first two-thirds of its height and then red for extra visibility, it boasts an elaborate and decorative lantern that is almost Middle Eastern in design, reminiscent of an exotic minaret. The simple keepers' cottages are close by and are still inhabited. The lighthouse is now open to the public.

Kereon lighthouse is situated near the Ile d'Ouessant at north Finistère. This light was largely privately financed by a member of the Kereon family in honour of her great-uncle, Charles-Marie Le Dall de Kereon, a nobleman and naval officer who was sent to the guillotine during the French Revolution in 1794.

Work on the Men Tensel (Gaelic for 'aggressive stone') reef began in 1907. The tower first showed its light in 1916, despite the problems of building during World War I, but the magnificent interior, made possible by the Kereon family, was installed after the war ended. The walls are beautifully panelled in Hungarian oak and the reception room floor has astonishing parquetry that appears almost three-dimensional from some angles.

The Ile d'Ouessant catches the full brunt of the north Atlantic and the very high seas are extremely dangerous. Before the grey granite circular tower and silver-grey lantern were constructed, many ships avoided the problem by using the Fromveur Passage. This stretch of water between the island and the mainland is full of reefs and rocks, making the journey almost as bad as staying on the open sea. Still inhabited, its keepers live in luxurious quarters compared to many – one of the bedrooms, walled and floored in oak, has a splendid boxed-in bed, also in oak.

Relief and supplies are still sent to Kereon by boat, where a hand winch operates a cork seat attached to a rope linking the tower to the boat. Vital materials are winched up first, in case high seas force the boat to leave before the relief keeper is winched up. The boat is tossed about on the ocean, as the keeper goes up the rope and is soaked with freezing cold water from the Atlantic. In the days before heating in lighthouses, it was almost impossible to dry clothes out in winter. Kereon today, however, has radiators and, once inside, life there is quite comfortable.

The Kereon lighthouse, France.

Portugal's coastline stretches for 2,730 miles,

but has only 25 lighthouses – the same number that illuminates the coast of Brittany alone. This may be explained by the Portuguese desire to keep their land to themselves – although they were at one time a proud maritime power, colonizing countries as diverse as Brazil, Macao, Goa, Guinea Bissau and Mozambique, they were also much invaded by Phoenicians, Moors, Vikings, Spanish and French armies.

In 1570 a wooden fortress was built at Bugio, at the mouth of the Tagus estuary leading to the capital, Lisbon. This was later replaced by a stone building but it did not show a light until 1775. The Spanish engineer Leonardo Turriano began work at Bugio in 1590 and his son, Joao, finished it in 1646. Taking 56 years to achieve, the Portuguese developed the first example of reef architecture over 150 years before the Stevensons or the Douglasses got going on their lighthouses in Scotland or England. In order to build the fort, which is 82 feet in diameter, they effectively had to build an island first. The reef was completely submerged at high tide and the stones had to be dovetailed using metal dowels and tar for caulking. The problem of erosion has meant that Bugio has been repaired and reinforced eight times, most recently in 1998. Automated in 1981, its light can be seen for 21 miles.

Cabo Mondego light was built much later, in 1857. Perched on the edge of a cliff, the tower is only 32 feet high, but is surrounded with handsome red-roofed buildings. The tower itself is stone and the lantern is topped in red. When it was first built, the light was fuelled by olive oil, and it is said that it used over 280,000 gallons every year.

Cabo de Sao Vicente also has the title of the oldest lighthouse in Portugal. In 1515, monks began to build a monastery and lit a fire to help passing seafarers. It expanded

Cabo Sao Vicente, Portugal.

during the next 300 years, and it was then decided to build a new tower with a huge light, first lit in 1846. Rising 88 feet, the tower stands on a cliff and is actually 282 feet above sea level, with a beacon that can be seen 32 miles away. Fully automated in 1982, the lighthouse is open to the public and the monastery is still inhabited.

Spain has many lighthouses. There are 54 around the north coast alone (more than twice as many as in the whole of Portugal), with 42 of them designated as major lighthouses – that is, visible for 20 or more nautical miles.

Bilbao, Spain's largest port, is located in the highly industrialized north, as are Gijon and El Ferrol. Here factories, refineries, mines and canning plants all rely on shipping to import materials and export products. The coast here is generally good for shipping – deep water close to steep cliffs, with no lethal rocks or reefs to worry about – so the lighthouses perform a different function to those of Britain, France or Portugal: their purpose is to point out capes and ports. They are also built differently. Where other lights have required amazing feats of engineering and years of dangerous work, Spanish lighthouses are usually built on breathtakingly beautiful sites with their lights and dwellings on a more domestic scale, perched high on a cliff or headland. Spain also has a piece of lighthouse history of which to be proud: the Torre de Hercules – the oldest working lighthouse in the world. Originally built by Gaius Sevius Lupus, it has stood and served for 1,900 years. Around 1285, it was shown on the Hereford Mappa Mundi with flames flaring from the top, and appears in many medieval manuscripts. However, there is no proof that it was actually lit between the end of the Roman Empire and the 17th century. The Tower of Hercules stands on a peninsula a couple of miles north of La Coruña and has seen four major renovations as well as many smaller repairs. In the late 15th century, its outer masonry and ramp were removed in order to make it an effective stronghold. In 1682, it was restored as a lighthouse and a wooden staircase was installed. The naval architect Don Eustaquio Giannini completely overhauled it in 1785 at the request of King Charles III of Spain. By this point, it was in a dilapidated condition and it took five years to rebuild the walls, encase them in granite and add a stone lantern fuelled with olive oil. The tower was raised again in 1847 and now stands 161 feet high.

Open to the public, it is a popular tourist destination, and visitors can read about its various transformations over the centuries from a bronze bas-relief. They can also see the smooth rock upon which Gaius Sevius Lupus carved his name, housed in a little stone building for protection. Although there is no remaining Roman work on the exterior of the tower, it is evident internally up to about 108 feet. Don Eustaquio Giannini made a very thoughtful and sensitive reconstruction, echoing and following the Roman design he found within. Today, of course, it is electrified and modernized, although still manned, and the beacon shines out with a range of 23 miles.

La Plata lighthouse in the Basque region can only be seen for 13 miles but it does, nevertheless, occupy a spectacular position, perched on a headland and marking the entrance to a narrow waterway leading to a commercial port. A fine, castellated building, it has the typical domed lantern so often seen on Spain's lighthouses – evidence of the Moorish influence noticeable in much Spanish architecture. Arab invaders conquered North Africa around 683 and brought Islam to the region. In due course, the Moors, of mixed Arab and Berber descent, crossed the water and established themselves and their civilization in Spain.

Above: La Coruña lighthouse, or Torre de Hercules.

Opposite: The rock of Gibraltar.

Also in Basque country is the very modern (1962) Cabo Villano tower at Gorliz. Visible 22 miles out to sea, it stands tall, white and elegant, 545 feet above sea level, with a shape reminiscent of a sophisticated cigarette lighter. Renovated in 1989, the tower is inhabited and the old foundations were once cannon placements for the defence of the coastline. The lighthouse on the Islas Cies could not be more different. A small, simple building at the apex of one of the two Cies islands, the 32-foot tall lighthouse actually stands 614 feet above the sea, and highlights the entrance to the important Galician port of Vigo. Although it is neither inhabited nor open to the public, it does have an extraordinarily steep and zigzagging road winding up to it.

On the south coast, in Andalucia, stands the Chipiona lighthouse. At 206 feet tall, it is one of Spain's highest towers as well as one of the most beautiful. Built in 1867 by Eduardo Saavedra, the tower has a splendid wrought-iron staircase and a house built around a beautiful interior courtyard. The courtyard, which is Moorish in design and protected by a glass pyramid, is typical of many houses in Morocco; they are built this way partly to keep the interior cool and partly to keep it private.

A little farther around the coast is Europa Point lighthouse, built in 1841 on the Rock of Gibraltar by the British Royal Engineers and painted white with a wide red band. It looks out over the strait to Morocco which, on a clear day, can be seen in the distance. At just 62 feet high and 160 feet above sea level, the tower is most noteworthy because of its location – on an English rock in the middle of Spain – and also because behind it stands the much taller and more graceful minaret of a nearby mosque, signifying the meeting of the two very different worlds of Europe and Africa.

Lighthouse on the Isla de Cies.

There can barely be a country in the world
with a coastline that does not have some sort of lighthouse or seamark. Iceland has a rugged coastline and is known throughout the world for its deep-sea fishing fleet. Icelandic people are as sturdy, independent and tough as the exceedingly harsh environment in which they live, and they pride themselves on their ability to cope with everything the elements can throw at them. Thus, the building of lighthouses around the country's shores was not a priority and indeed the very first one, in Reykjanes, was only erected in 1878. Iceland became an independent country in 1918, with any lighthouses predating this constructed under the aegis of the Danish lighthouse authority, who had plenty of experience.

As early as 1561, a timber structure was built at Anholt in Denmark to mark the narrow sound between Denmark and southern Sweden, and by 1624 Nidingen (now in Sweden) had a double light to distinguish it from the Anholt light. Norway, too, had its early lighthouses, such as the first one built in 1665 at Lindesnes. There is also Kvitsoy, which began as a private business in 1700 when the king granted permission for a beacon there. The huge tower at Kvitsoy today is a replacement built by the government in 1829.

Early in the 20th century, Danish engineer Thorvald Krabbe became Iceland's first lighthouse commissioner. Until then, Icelandic lights were built following the architectural traditions of other nations, but the country soon developed its own style. The lights tend to have tapered, round towers, although occasionally they are square, with a balustrade at the top surrounding the lantern, which is usually smaller than the diameter of the tower itself and smaller than the lanterns in the rest of Europe and North America. In fact, many of the towers themselves are rather short and squat, but the

Top: **A castellated lighthouse, Iceland.**

Bottom: **Stykkisholmur, Iceland.**

BEACONS BEYOND

major difference is their colour. Because the land is under snow and ice for much of the year, they are usually painted yellow or orange to boost visibility.

In 1996 the Icelandic Maritime Administration was formed, which takes care of 104 lighthouses and employs about 100 staff. Iceland's lighthouses are automated and lighthouse keepers are no longer needed, but the beacons still assist mariners who negotiate the rocky shores and narrow fjords. There are three splendid, cheerful little lighthouses at Krossnes, Hoskuldsey and Klofnings, which are all an identical bright orange. Short and square with small windows, they have rather elegant balustrades surrounding the small, octagonal, peaked lanterns. Standing against the whiteness of virgin snow and the extraordinarily luminous water, they bring an unexpected gaiety to an otherwise severe and monochromatically beautiful landscape.

At Suourflos, near the port of Akranes, two unusual lighthouses light the way. The first, built during World War I, is an elegantly proportioned rectangular building. The base and top of the tower are of equal size, while the central section is narrower. Scrap metal was used for the balustrade and the lantern. On the opposite side of the water stands a newer tower, built during World War II, and it could not be more different. Tall, tapering and circular, with tiny windows all the way up, it has an unusual balustrade and an even more unusual set of buttresses around the base. The first lighthouse is reminiscent of classical architecture; the second is almost rocket shaped.

The tiny little lighthouse that stands guard at the entrance to Stykkisholmur Harbour is actually just a lantern. Built in the late 19th century, it was originally the lantern for Grotta lighthouse, but as it is now sited on the level, its beacon is highly visible at night and its bright colour makes it an excellent daymark as well.

On the south coast of the Netherlands is an unusual high light (a low light stands on the shore nearby): Westkapelle high light, established in 1815, is just a lantern with a modern optic at the top of a rather ornate church tower. In Germany, the Bremerhaven light was built in 1854 by the well-known architect Simon Loschen, who deliberately designed his Neo-Gothic tower to look like a church. Originally the light was fuelled by rapeseed oil, then by natural gas and, since 1925, by electricity.

As the western colonial powers expanded their empires, trade grew, and more and more people travelled to distant lands, including colonizers, colonists, convicts and adventurers. Ships took people and equipment and returned with precious cargoes, but unfortunately many came to grief on unlit shores using badly drawn charts. More lighthouses were needed and, by the mid-19th century, they began to get them.

In 1864 the United States, Britain, Sweden, France, Netherlands, Belgium, Austria, Italy and Spain made a treaty with the sultan of Morocco to construct a lighthouse near Tangiers, in northern Morocco, at Cap Spartel where the Atlantic meets the Mediterranean. The sultan agreed to carry the cost of building the lighthouse, and the other countries would pay the running costs. This was probably among the earliest lighthouses on the coast of Africa (excluding the Pharos at Alexandria).

Travelling from Europe to Australia, traders could pick up the lights of France and Spain before hitting the south Atlantic. They would also pass lighthouses such as Cap Vert light on the Pointe des Almadies, near Dakar in Senegal, built by the French on the westernmost point of Africa in 1864. Still active this is said to be the most powerful light in Africa. Finally, they would see the light of Cape Agulhas on the southern tip of Africa, built by the Portuguese in 1849, and know it was the last time they would see land for a long time.

By the late 1880s, those travellers would have been thrilled to see the beacon of the lighthouse at Cape Leeuwin, built on the south-west tip of Australia, south of Perth, having sailed through the Indian Ocean for weeks. Prior to that, there were already lights erected in the Bass Strait between Australia and Tasmania, the first being Cape Otway lighthouse on the mainland, which was built in 1848.

The Australian authorities began building lighthouses in the early 19th century, and their best-known architect in New South Wales was Francis Howard Greenway, a Bristol man who was awaiting execution in England when his sentence was commuted to transportation to New South Wales. Lachlan Macquarie, the new governor, decided upon a programme of public works, and one of his first projects was to build a lighthouse on the southern tip of Sydney Harbour, using Greenway as his architect and other convicts as workers. Built of local sandstone, the Macquarie light first shone out in 1818. Greenway warned the governor that the sandstone was soft and would not stand the test of time, and within a few years iron bands had to be placed around the tower to stop it from crumbling. Greenway died impoverished in the late 1830s, but his designs were used in 15 lighthouses in New South Wales. In 1863 the Macquarie light was on the point of collapse, when the authorities built an almost exact copy of the original: what we can see today.

Until 1869 when the Suez Canal was opened to link the Mediterranean to the Red Sea, ships from Europe making for India and the Middle and Far East would have rounded the Cape of Good Hope and made their way up the east coast of Africa, and either up to Saudi Arabia and Persia through the Arabian Sea or across the Indian Ocean to India itself. The Suez Canal is 101 miles long, but saved mariners thousands of miles and long weeks of sailing time and must have seemed like a miracle. Travelling the long way around, they

Top: **Cape Leeuwin, Australia.**

Bottom: **Tierra del Fuego.**

would have seen beacons shining at Alleppey in Kerala in south-west India, and the lighthouse built on Great Basses Reef off the southern tip of India in 1878. This was built of Scottish granite, quarried and cut there, then carried more than 10,000 nautical miles to its future home. Depending on the final destination, they might have seen Dondra Head light at the southern tip of Sri Lanka, an elegant, octagonal stone and brick building erected in 1889. Standing 177 feet tall and surrounded by palm trees, it is amazing that its designer was Sir James Douglass, chief engineer of Trinity House in England.

Passengers and goods leaving from North America for far-off shores had a different set of problems – namely the famously ferocious weather conditions around Cape Horn at the southern tip of South America. Until the Panama Canal was built in 1914 to link the Atlantic to the Pacific Ocean, that was the only route to Australasia or Japan. Brazil has a large number of lighthouses, and all the active ones are owned by the navy, many of which are fairly modern enclosed towers made of concrete and fibreglass. The larger towers are manned either by resident keepers or rotating naval staff and very few are open to the public. In the early days, travellers would have been lucky to see a light in Uruguay but now it has seven lighthouses, built in the late 19th and early 20th centuries. The 194-foot high tapered concrete tower on the Isla de Lobos is not only Uruguay's highest, but also one of the highest of its kind in the world. Sailing south, there was the beacon of the Punta Mogote light at Mar del Plata, Argentina, marking the stretch of coast to the south of the River Plate and Buenos Aires, built in 1891.

Tierra del Fuego has a lighthouse, known romantically as 'the lighthouse at the end of the world', at its southern tip. Argentina has 80 lights on its rocky shores, Chile has over 100, Peru and Ecuador both have almost 40 and Colombia has more than 50.

Opposite: **Bremerhaven, Germany.**

Far right: **Westkapelle lighthouse, the Netherlands.**

One of the many wonderful things about lighthouses is the enormous differences to be seen in their design. Considering that all that is really needed is a tall structure with a powerful light at the top, it is fascinating to see the individual styles that architects and indeed countries come up with. It is not just a question of a stone structure versus an iron one, or a rock tower versus an exposed screw-pile light: it is somehow more personal than that. Compare La Entallada light in the Canary Islands – a most peculiar brown stone building faced with white latticework that looks like dead coral or honeycomb – with the privately built Playa del Carmen in Mexico, with its fairground, helterskelter appearance. Look also at the difference between Sand Key lighthouse in Florida (1853), an exposed, screw-pile structure with black legs and white lantern, and Cape Lookout light in North Carolina (1859), a soaring brick tower with unusual black and white diamond pattern paintwork. These differences reveal the thought and love that has gone into every single one of these beacons of light, that are there to help humankind find its way safely back to shore from the seven-eighths of this world that is water.

INDEX

ACKNOWLEDGEMENTS:

All photographs have been reproduced courtesy of Alamy with the exception of the following:

Corbis U.K. Limited /Yann Arthus-Bertrand 133; /Jean Gulchard 92, 118, 121, 125; /Joseph Sohm, Visions of America 138 bottom.